D. E. HOSTE
A Prince with God

D. E. HOSTE
A Prince with God

*Hudson Taylor's Successor
as General Director of
the China Inland Mission
1900 - 1935*

BY PHYLLIS THOMPSON

Foreword by
Bishop Frank Houghton

Shoals, Indiana

D. E. Hoste: A Prince with God

Published by Kingsley Press
PO Box 973
Shoals, IN 47581
USA

Tel. (800) 971-7985
www.kingsleypress.com
E-mail: sales@kingsleypress.com

ISBN: 978-1-937428-64-8 (paperback)
ISBN: 978-1-937428-65-5 (ebook)

First Kingsley Press edition 2017

First published in 1947 by China Inland Mission

This first Kingsley Press edition is complete and unabridged. Grammar and punctuation has been updated to conform to the house style of the publisher.

Contents

Foreword 7
Preface 9
1. Early Years 11
2. The Cambridge Seven 23
3. First Impressions 33
4. Hungtung 45
5. Preparation of a Leader 55
6. Marriage and Furlough 67
7. Leader of the Mission 81
8. Building on the Foundations 97
9. Spiritual Leadership 107
10. The Man Himself 117
11. The Forward Movement 127
12. That Which Remained 139
13. Extracts from Letters 147
14. Selected Writings 173

Foreword

No one who is separated to the gospel of God as D. E. Hoste was can fail to profit by the reading of this book. He was chosen to be leader in the work of the China Inland Mission because he had served the people of China and his fellow missionaries in a spirit of love, humility, and self-discipline. Writing to Hudson Taylor from Shansi after less than a year in China, he asks prayer for help in language study and in getting to know the people. "More and more I see," he says, "that there will be need of much love and forbearance and willingness to be the inferior, if one is really to get across the gulf there is between us." By God's grace, these qualities were manifest in his life and so he succeeded in bridging the gulf.

Exactly the same qualities are required in missionaries in China sixty years later. How relevant, for instance, are Mr. Hoste's words of counsel concerning our relation to the people around us! He admits that "close contact with people of a different civilization" may involve trial, but "there is danger lest we draw back from that contact, thus failing to pay the full price of a truly Christ-like relationship with those around." "It will not avail much to preach to the Chinese of access to God through the blood of Jesus if they find that there is not access to the missionary himself and his home."

The other main lesson of Mr. Hoste's life, so it seems to me, is equally vital for our own day. I refer to his prayerfulness. He had noted how, by the grace of God, Hudson Taylor was prepared to yield temporarily to opposition or criticism even when the course of action which he proposed was "intrinsically sound and beneficial." But he had proved that "it is possible to move men, through God, by prayer alone," and so eventually his suggestions were accepted, his vision realized. "By prayer alone" – this is a method which applies to the whole work of the Mission, and not merely to the provision of material supplies. "Patient, persevering prayer," wrote Mr. Hoste, "plays a more vital and practical part in the development of the Mission's work than most people have any idea of." "Lord, teach us to pray" – not to talk about praying, to formulate a philosophy of prayer, or to analyze its effects, but actually to pray as Hudson Taylor did, as D. E. Hoste did. The record of their lives is of little or no value to us unless we "imitate their faith."

Frank Houghton

Preface

My sincere thanks are due to all who so readily contributed character studies and personal stories of Mr. Hoste. Without them the difficult task of writing the biographical sketch would have been impossible, for Mr. Hoste had already retired when I first arrived in China, and I did not know him personally. No diaries and very few personal letters of his have come to light, and I have therefore been almost entirely dependent on those who have known him through the years for any information about his life and character.

It has not been easy to present a true picture of Mr. Hoste. He was evidently a man who had few intimates and was to an unusual degree "separated unto God." Yet to depict him only as a saintly man of prayer and ignore the human idiosyncrasies and weaknesses from which he was by no means immune would have been unreal.

I should also like to express my gratitude to the Rev. H. W. Oldham, Mr. Stanley Houghton, Mr. David Bentley-Taylor, Mr. Gordon Martin and others who have been kind enough to read through the manuscript at various stages of its development, and make suggestions and corrections. Most of all, Mr. Norman Baker deserves mention, for most of the material on which I had to work was collected by him, and his prayerful interest and help have been deeply appreciated.

This very inadequate tribute to our late leader goes forth with the prayer that, in spite of its many deficiencies, the Spirit of God may nevertheless work through one who, being dead, yet speaketh.

Phyllis Thompson
June, 1947

Chapter 1

Early Years

DIXON Edward Hoste was born on July 23rd, 1861, just four years before the formation of the China Inland Mission. He came of soldier stock. His father was a major-general in the Royal Artillery, and his grandfather was Colonel Sir George Hoste, C.B., at one time Gentleman Usher to Queen Victoria. From his earliest childhood, therefore, the little boy became accustomed to a life in which personal interests were secondary to the claims of king and country. As his father moved from one military appointment to another, so the family was uprooted from surroundings which had become familiar, and transferred into those which were new and strange. Military precision characterized the household, and in spite of the strain which constant moves must have imposed upon the parents of a growing family, order and discipline soon prevailed as they settled down in each new home. Everyone had his place, and everything its niche; and in the shortest possible time the accustomed routine was observed as though it had never been disturbed.

Major-General Hoste and his wife were God-fearing people, and the instruction of their children in sound Scriptural principles was to them a matter of primary importance. The mother, in particular, was a born teacher, and as one of her sons wrote of her many years later, "to have passed through her hands was to have a knowledge of the Bible almost from end to end implanted on the mind for life. Whatever the special lessons, the main ideas were of God's love to us revealed in the Lord Jesus Christ, our own sins and shortcomings, together with our need of a personal repentance and renewal; while the thought that we had been sent into the world to do some work for God and man was never far away."

They were taught also to remember the needs of foreign missions, notably that of the Church Missionary Society, and for D. E. Hoste this resulted in a lifelong "feeling of interest and attachment," as he himself said, "towards that truly great Society."

In such favorable surroundings, therefore, it might reasonably be supposed that his childhood would be a very happy one, but this was not so. To more than one friend in later years he admitted that he had "no joy in childhood – no joy at all." While he did not elucidate that remark, the reason for his unhappiness evidently lay in himself. From a child he had an unusually reserved and sensitive temperament; it would seem that he had no close and intimate relationships, even with the members of his own family. He had an elder brother and sister, and seven other children were born after him, yet his disposition was more like that so often found in an only child than in one of a large family. He could not express himself freely and naturally, and even his parents found him difficult to understand.

When he was about eight years of age, the thought of the future life caused him deep concern, and had he gone to his mother in his inward distress, he might have been early led to the one who came to seek and to save that which was lost. Apparently, however, he kept his anxiety shut up within him, and gradually the deep impression made by the fear of eternal punishment faded from his conscious thoughts.

He went to school at Clifton College, and, away from the softer influences of a Christian home, became increasingly careless about his soul's welfare. Very little is known about his schooldays beyond the fact that the character of the principal, Dr. Percival, who later became Bishop of Hereford, won his lifelong admiration and approval. Of the training he received he said in later years, "One thing about it – it was thorough and has stood me in good stead all my life."

T. E. Brown, the poet, was on the staff of Clifton in those days, and his mastery of the wide range of English poetry made a lasting impression on D. E. Hoste. In those schooldays he learned by heart many long passages of English poetry, especially Shakespeare, which he could still repeat sixty years later, and loved to dwell on in times of leisure.

As a scholar he was diligent, and did well in his examinations. Before he was nine he was reading Greek! His personal life, however, was an unhappy one. It is not difficult to imagine the self-defensive veneer of aloofness that he would adopt, and the construction his more spontaneous fellow-scholars would put on it. In later years he told a friend, "I had a nightmare of a time at school." Yet it was probably the very isolation of those early years that helped to develop his unusual powers of concentration, accurate appraisal of character, and the ability to take a balanced and dispassionate view of a complex situation. Perhaps here, too, was the place where he obtained his sympathy for the underdog!

At the age of seventeen he entered the Royal Military Academy at Woolwich. On one of the stained-glass windows of the hall where the young cadets assembled for prayers and meals were the words, "Through obedience learn to command." Prompt and unquestioning obedience, erect carriage, precision and tidiness were amongst the things which he learned; and his later experience in the wise and just treatment of men proved invaluable training for the life-work for which God was preparing him.

When he was eighteen he was commissioned as a lieutenant in his father's regiment, the Royal Artillery. For three years he led a completely irreligious life, "entirely indifferent," to use his own words, "to the claims of God." Only the pleadings and warnings in his mother's letters occasionally disturbed his peace of mind and caused him a little uneasiness. Then, deep in his heart, the conviction that the Bible was true and that he himself was deliberately walking the road that leads to destruction would reassert itself, only to be quickly stifled again as he set himself to make a success of the career that lay before him. He even ceased to pray, though accustomed to it from early childhood, for he realized that to do so when he was turning away from God would be mockery.

The worldly young officer, however, was unable to resist the gentle persistence of the Holy Spirit's working in his heart. In the year 1882, he began to feel dissatisfied with the life he was leading, and there came a constantly-recurring desire to be of some real use in the world. Impressions gained from the teaching received in his childhood could not be wholly forgotten, and now they came again to his mind. While conscious of the desire towards a nobler life than that lived for the gratification of his own inclinations, he knew full well what was involved in becoming a disciple of the Lord Jesus Christ. It meant a complete and unreserved surrender of the whole life. It meant placing himself absolutely at the disposal of God. He felt that the cost was greater than he was prepared to pay.

He was stationed in the Isle of Wight at the time, and towards the end of the year went to stay with his parents in Brighton, where they had retired. The time was drawing near when he was to make the most important decision any man or woman can make. In various ways the fact that God was seeking him became evident. One day, as he was walking along the promenade, a woman handed him a tract; and whatever his reactions at the time, the incident made a deep impression on him. His brother William, an undergraduate at Cambridge, had recently come under the influence of the American evangelists, Moody and Sankey, and he longed that Dixon should share his new-found joy in the Lord Jesus.

The young officer, however, was still adamant in his unwillingness to surrender; and when the two evangelists, under whose soul-stirring singing and powerful preaching hundreds were being led to Christ, came to hold a mission in Brighton, he refused to attend the meetings.

One evening, as he sat reading, his mother came and once more urged him to accompany her and some of the other members of the family to the meeting. He again declined, although he realized that he was disappointing her, and he settled down to read the evening paper. His elder brother, William, remained behind with him; but when the others had gone he got up and said quietly, "Come on, Dick. Put on your wraps and go with me to the meeting." There was a strange compulsion in his voice, and D. E. Hoste, putting down the paper, arose and accompanied his brother without demur.

It was late when they arrived at the Dome, where the meetings were being held, and it was with a sense of relief that he saw that the only seats left were at the back of the hall. Enthusiastic singing was already in progress, led by a large choir. On the platform sat a number of clergymen. The young officer looked at them, wondering which one was Moody. He felt quite unmoved.

After a time, a man dressed as an ordinary businessman came on to the speaker's platform from a rear entrance. From the moment he took his place there, D. E. Hoste seemed unable to take his eyes off him. There was something different about this man. He walked quickly to one of those seated on the platform, and bent his head to speak to him. Then he turned to the choir leader and asked him to lead in the singing of a certain hymn. When that was over, he stepped into the middle of the platform, and said quietly, "Let us pray."

Never before had D. E. Hoste heard such a prayer. Moody *talked* to God. He talked as though God was there, as though he knew him, as a man talks to a friend. He talked as though God could be depended upon to do his work in men's hearts right then and there.

Prayer over, the unconventional, earnest American on the platform opened his Bible and read a passage; then he began to preach. From the moment he started to speak, said D. E. Hoste afterwards, the Spirit of God began to work in his heart. He was convinced, convicted. His soul was stirred to its very depths. The effect of the meeting upon him can best be described in his own words:

"As Mr. Moody with intense earnestness and directness preached the solemn truths concerning God's judgment of the impenitent and ungodly, and seriously warned his hearers to flee from the wrath to come, a deep sense of my sinful and perilous state laid hold of my soul with great power. On the other hand, the realization of what it would cost to turn from the associations and habits of the life I was then living and the knowledge that I should be exposed to the opposition, ridicule, and dislike of my worldly companions, held me back from definite decision for Christ. During the next fortnight a fierce conflict was waged in my heart and mind."

Such a conflict could not continue indefinitely. The issue must be faced and a choice made. On the last evening of the mission, seated at the back of the hall, he felt overwhelmingly conscious of the sin of his ungodly life. At the same time, he was seized by a conviction that he must be saved now or never. The moment had come. Realizing his guilt before God, he knelt down and placed himself without any reservations at the disposal of the Lord Jesus, thankfully receiving the salvation offered so freely through the sacrifice on Calvary. There came to him such a sense of the graciousness of the Lord he had resisted so long in immediately forgiving and receiving him that his heart was won. His whole being was filled with new life; a deep joy possessed his soul. And his mother, who did not even know that he was at the meeting, saw with amazement the upright figure of her soldier son making his way up the aisle in open confession of his Savior.

To those who observe these things, the miracle of the new birth must ever be a source of wonder. The one who drinks at last from the wells of salvation finds that from the very spring of his being the course of his whole life is altered. The change is outward only because it is first inward. D. E. Hoste, who had neglected Bible reading for years, now found that it was almost the only book he desired to read. Its revelations gripped him, and he saw that the natural desires and aims of man were as trifles and fleeting shadows in the light of eternity. To make known the truths of God among men seemed to him to be of far greater importance than any other occupation. "If this gospel is true," he thought, "and I know it is, as it has changed my life, I want to make it known where Christ is not known. There are many people in other lands who have never heard it, and the Lord wants them to hear it, for he says so. *I want to give my life to this.*"

It was not long before he expressed this desire to his father, and suggested that he should resign his commission in the Royal Artillery. His father, however, while rejoicing in the salvation and zeal of his son, refused permission for him to do this, pointing out from the depth of his longer experience that the spiritual joy he was now feeling might diminish. It would be wiser to take no important step rashly, lest it should afterwards be regretted. The young man, disappointed though he was, recognized the wisdom of the warning. More than that, he believed the hand of God to be behind his parent's restraining influence. He decided, therefore, that he would not broach the matter again, but rather give himself to prayer, trusting the Lord to influence his father's mind according to his own will.

Shortly after this he returned to his battery in the Isle of Wight. Here one of the first important tests in his spiritual life awaited him. It is one thing to be profoundly stirred by the need of the souls of those dying in heathen darkness, and to feel prepared to make any sacrifice to take the gospel to them; it is another thing to acknowledge Christ as Savior and Lord among companions who will probably regard such a profession with disconcerting indifference or open scorn. D. E. Hoste determined to make known his position as a Christian without delay, and with inward trepidation asked his commanding officer if he could see him privately.

"Well, what is it?" asked the officer when they were alone in his room. He was not unaccustomed to young subalterns coming to him when they were in some sort of scrape, and probably wondered what Hoste had been up to!

"I wanted to tell you, sir, that I've become a Christian."

"A – a *what?*" He started visibly.

"A Christian, sir."

"Oh!" There was a note of anxiety rather than of interest in his voice. He looked towards the mantelpiece, on which were a number of invitations to mess dinners. "I suppose that means you won't be coming to any more of them?" he asked, waving his hand towards the invitation cards. His mess was a small one already, and he could ill afford to have it further reduced in number at such functions by the absence of even one! But he accepted the position with philosophical resignation, and the young lieutenant withdrew, thankful that the interview had not proved as difficult as he had feared – and to muse on the unexpected reaction of his senior! His conversion, indeed, seems to have caused no great stir amongst his companions, and he said afterwards that he got on quite well amongst them until he was baptized. "And that," he remarked, "was the end of me!"

One at least, however, of his fellow officers never forgot him. The late Brigadier-General A. H. Adair, who was a fellow subaltern with D. E. Hoste, wrote of him in 1946:

"He taught me my duties in a very pleasant way, and I discovered at once that I was dealing with no ordinary young man. We were only soldiering together for a few months, but those few months made an impression on me which has lasted a lifetime. One could not but be struck by his most earnest convictions, which I felt deep respect for – and which to this day I reverence. My recollection is that he was on fire with it all, and that he really never thought of anything else. He spent all his spare time studying the Bible, and in teaching and preaching on the beach and elsewhere."

At the time of his conversion he was a habitual smoker. No one had ever suggested to him that smoking might be inconsistent with the Christian life, and as the habit gave him some satisfaction, he continued it.

"One day," he told a friend some years later, "I was in my room, tilted back in my chair with my open Bible before me. I had begun thoroughly to enjoy the Word of God. As I read, I smoked, and raised my head occasionally to blow the tobacco smoke over the open pages before me. All at once the thought came to me: 'Is this honoring to God, for me to sit reading his Word and indulging in a selfish habit as I am doing?' I could not dismiss this impression from my mind. I felt that nothing should come between me and my Lord. I at once stopped smoking, and from that moment have never touched tobacco."

His new desires brought him in touch with new people. Before very long he had formed friendships with Christians in the neighborhood, and with them took his part in open-air witnessing. His brother William had also found like-minded friends at Cambridge. One of these, in particular, was becoming increasingly interested in the missionary cause in China, and it was probably through Montagu Beauchamp that D. E. Hoste first had his attention drawn, early in 1883, to the literature of that young and comparatively unknown society, the China Inland Mission. Referring to that time many years later, he wrote:

"I became deeply impressed by the single-hearted, self-denying devotion to the cause of the gospel in China which characterized the writing of Mr. Hudson Taylor and others. The lines of simple and direct faith in God for temporal supply and protection, and also the close identification of the missionaries with the Chinese, in social ways adapting themselves to Chinese customs and habits, commended themselves greatly to me. The combination of firm and clear grasp of fundamental truth with a wide and tolerant spirit in regard to ecclesiastical distinctions which is a special feature of the Mission, drew out my sympathy, while the overwhelming spiritual need of the Chinese began to burden my heart."

Well might he be burdened by the thought of the land in which millions of souls passed yearly into eternity without ever hearing of Christ! Who could read, *China: Its Spiritual Need and Claims* and not feel a surge of shame at the apathy of the Christian church in leaving that great empire so long without the gospel? It was as though a consuming fire burned within Hudson Taylor when he prepared that little book which did so much to awaken Christians to a sense of responsibility towards the Chinese; and his words, simple and sincere, seemed to burn themselves into the minds of those who read. It is not difficult to imagine the intensity with which the young lieutenant, whose heart was becoming increasingly sensitive to eternal realities by the daily exercise of prayer and Bible study, would slowly read and ponder such words as these:

"Were all the subjects of the court of Pekin marshalled in single rank and file, allowing one yard between man and man, they would encircle the globe more than ten times at its Equator. Were they to march past the spectator at the rate of thirty miles a day, they would move on and on, day after day, week after week, month after month; and more than twenty-three and a half years would elapse before the last individual had passed by. Estimating the number of converts of all the Protestant missions in China at 3,000, the whole of them would pass by in less than an hour and a half of that twenty-three and a half years. Mournful and impressive fact – such is the proportion of those who are journeying heavenward to those whose downward course can but lead to everlasting woe! Four hundred millions of souls, 'having no hope, and without God in the world!' ... Among so vast a population the number of deaths continually occurring is necessarily very great. It is stated that the daily mortality of China is 33,000! Think of it – a mortality which in less than three months exceeds the whole population of huge, overgrown London – which in a year and a half exceeds the total number of the inhabitants of our highly-favored England. Let the reader realize it if he can, for the thought is overwhelming. And can the Christians of England sit still with folded arms while these multitudes are perishing – perishing for lack of knowledge – for lack of that knowledge which England possesses so richly, which has made England what England is, and has made us what we are?

"Dear brethren and sisters, think of the imperative command of our great Captain and Leader, 'Go ye into all the world, and preach the gospel to every creature'; think of the millions upon millions of poor benighted China to whom no loving follower of the self-renouncing one has 'brought good tidings of good,' or 'published salvation,' and weigh well the fearful words: 'If thou forbear to deliver them that are drawn unto death, and those that are ready to be slain; if thou sayest, Behold, we knew it not; doth not he that pondereth the heart consider it? and he that keepeth thy soul, doth not he know it? and shall not he render to every man according to his works?'"

The mighty pressure of the one who so loved the world that he gave his only Son was upon D. E. Hoste, and now that his mind was so definitely directed towards China, the purpose of God for his life became more evident. In May he received a letter from his father saying that if he still desired to be a missionary, he could now feel free to resign his commission.

The path God had chosen seemed to be opening up before him, but still he proceeded cautiously. It was not until July that he wrote to the London office of the China Inland Mission, asking for more detailed information about the work, and offering himself as a candidate.

On the day his application was received the Mission sustained a heavy loss to its ranks by the death of Dr. Harold Schofield. This single-hearted, brilliant man, who had obtained seven degrees, and before whom lay a career of unusual promise, had gladly turned away from the prospect of worldly success in order to serve the Lord in China. He had been there only three years when he contracted typhus fever and died – but not before he had prayed, often and earnestly, that the best men in *all* respects, mentally, educationally as well as spiritually, should be sent to China. Was it merely coincidence that on the very day of his death the application of D. E. Hoste, first of the famous "Cambridge Seven" to seek entrance to the Mission, should be received? Or was it just another proof, sealed by its very timing, that God answers prayer?

It was eventually arranged for Lieutenant Hoste to meet Hudson Taylor, and so it came about that one day in August he walked along Pyrland Road, with its two rows of conventional, four-storied basement houses, and, mounting the steps to the front door of No. 6, rang the bell. In a few minutes he was standing face to face with the man whose zeal and devotion had impressed him so deeply.

If we could draw back the curtain of time, and look not only into the rather shabby little room at the Mission's headquarters, but also into the hearts of the genial, middle-aged man and the respectful, reserved young officer as they met for that first interview, what should we see? Had Hudson Taylor any prophetic instinct which told him that here stood his Joshua, the man who was to lead on when he himself must lay down his responsibilities? And as he listened to the leader of the small but growing Mission, had Dixon Hoste any premonition that in less than twenty years he himself would be occupying that position? It seems not. The future was hidden from them. All we know of that first interview is that Hudson Taylor spoke frankly to the intending candidate of the dangers and difficulties of missionary work in China. He told him of the isolation, of being separated, often by many weeks' journey, from fellow workers; of the privations, hard living conditions, and lack of privacy. He did not minimize the suspicions with which foreigners were regarded by the Chinese people, and the humiliations to which missionaries must be prepared to submit. And not the least difficult thing to endure, he pointed out, was the contempt with which fellow countrymen regarded the Englishman who identified himself with the Chinese by living amongst them as one of themselves.

At the conclusion of the interview Hudson Taylor advised the young man before him to continue to wait, quietly and prayerfully, for God to confirm his will, and to take no further step immediately. This he was willing to do, for he felt an even greater veneration than before for the man with whom he had just been speaking. His enthusiasm, however, had been quickened rather than damped by what he had heard; and as he walked away he realized that his heart was more than ever set upon becoming a missionary in China.

Chapter 2

The Cambridge Seven

For the second time D. E. Hoste was checked in his desire to go to China. At first his father's refusal to allow him to resign his commission had seemed the only obstacle to be overcome. When the faith manifested in his patient waiting for God to work was rewarded, there appeared to be no further confirmation needed that it was indeed the divine will for him to go forward. Hudson Taylor's apparent uncertainty as to whether God had really called him, however, meant that he must reconsider the whole matter. As he did so, it was impressed upon him how high a privilege it was to be called to be a missionary. Of all vocations, surely none could be greater than that of proclaiming the good news of salvation from sin and its awful penalty to those who had never yet heard of Jesus Christ! No fear of the personal sacrifice involved appears to have occurred to him, nor even misgivings as to his own ability to fulfil the commission. To the one who loves there is joy in sacrifice; and if God calls, will he not also enable? D. E. Hoste was not seriously apprehensive on either of those points. He was, however, afraid of presumption. To quote his own words, "I felt more and more the need of the utmost care and caution, lest I should presume to enter so privileged a life and service as that of a missionary in inland China, without having been really called and appointed thereto by the Lord." In his uncertainty, he discussed the matter with various Christian friends. It must have caused him considerable inward conflict to hear the opinion again and again expressed that he should remain in the Army! The reasons given, however, never appeared to him conclusive, and, like many another in a similar position, he was forced back upon God, who alone could give him the assurance he was seeking.

The "Cambridge Seven" soon after arrival in China

How that assurance eventually came, we do not know. Occasionally he was able to attend the Saturday afternoon prayer meeting at the headquarters of the China Inland Mission in Pyrland Road, and the fellowship and prayer of others whose great concern was the spread of the gospel in China provided a spiritual atmosphere altogether congenial to him. Through his friendship with Montagu Beauchamp, he also met other young men at Cambridge upon whose hearts the need of China was becoming an increasing burden. No doubt contact with such kindred spirits did much to strengthen and encourage his hope that God would grant him his desire.

In February, 1884, he went before the council of the China Inland Mission, and even at this stage he seems to have been uncertain as to God's purpose for him. An extract from the minutes of that meeting reads "D. E. Hoste interviewed by council. Interview somewhat informal, as Mr. Hoste not quite clear as to his future, but hoping that ultimately he might be able to work in China."

The fear of self-willed action which characterized his later life and service was manifest in his slowness now to take the very step he most desired to take. It was a deep distrust in his own impulses and motives, rather than any lack of faith in God which held him back, and not until May did he finally resign his commission. Whether he obtained some special indication of God's will before he did so is not known, but it seems more probable that the step had to be taken more in obedience to the inward pressure upon his spirit than in response to any direct revelation.

Hudson Taylor had suggested that he should get some experience in Christian work, so during the next few months he spent some time working among enquirers in connection with the great evangelistic campaign held in London by Moody and Sankey. Those were days of spiritual revival, when men and women were coming under deep conviction of sin, and the experience he gained in dealing with souls in distress was invaluable for his future ministry. This was not the only preparation he made for missionary service, however. A younger brother, in his early teens at the time, has recollections of an even more important spiritual equipment.

"I do not remember what exact steps were taken to prepare my brother for his future work, but the impression I have is that a very important part of it was undertaken by himself, in acts of severe self-discipline, in a very strict watch over his thoughts, words, and deeds, and in the expression of a deep regret when he felt that he had stated his own opinions too strongly, or had allowed his temper to get the upper hand in any way. I think, too, that in those days he often went out of his way to undertake tasks which, by reason of a certain natural shyness, must have been difficult and distasteful to him. In the early days of which I am speaking, he was rather especially fastidious, and anything in the way of dirt or smells he found very trying. I will leave others to say how far it was possible for one living and travelling in China in the eighties and nineties to avoid such things; but I believe that in his passionate desire to work for God amongst the Chinese, my brother deliberately schooled himself to face and to put up with all such discomforts. It was in ways such as these and in the constant practice of prayer and Bible study that I think the principal part of his preparation lay."

The same brother has also memories of quite another order. When he broke through his inherent reserve, D. E. Hoste could be gay and light-hearted, a delightful companion to schoolboys, as the following reminiscence reveals:

"There stands out in my memory a very happy holiday that two of us younger boys spent under his care at Sandown, in the Isle of Wight. I think my parents must have planned it with the thought of the training and experience it would be for him, as well as for the enjoyment it would afford us. For indeed it must have been a business for a young man of three or four and twenty to find rooms, to cope with a landlady, to lay out to the best advantage the funds provided, to arrange for our amusement and to look after our health. Under this last head I remember an iron rule that in no circumstances were we to bathe more than six times in any one day!

He took us about the island, and wherever we went he had something to tell us about what we were to see or some story to relate suggested by it. I remember his taking us one day to see a fort where he had been at one time quartered in his military days. As we went round it he gave a dramatic turn to the proceedings by assuming to himself the part of his former commanding officer, who, it appeared, had been strict, not to say irascible; while we two small ones found ourselves in the role he had once filled of the junior officers responsible for the military smartness of the premises. Wherever we went there was something wrong! I can see him now in a last explosion of wrath just as we were leaving the fort, when his eye fell on some small weeds in an obscure corner of the parade ground. It was clear, he said, as he attacked them with his stick, that young officers who could allow the whole place to be grown over with vegetation in this disgraceful manner had no idea at all of their duty! And so, with much merriment, we quitted the fort."

In the autumn he applied again to the Mission and was accepted on condition that his testimonials were satisfactory. While those who have the responsibility of accepting or refusing candidates spend much time seeking the Lord to know his will concerning each one, they do not neglect the means at their disposal for appraising the character and qualifications of those who apply. Two or three people who have known the applicants personally are therefore approached, in order that as balanced and impartial an opinion as possible may be formed of their suitability for missionary work.

So it came about that one day the Rev. W. T. Storrs of Sandown, Isle of Wight, found a letter from the China Inland Mission in his mail.

China Inland Mission
6 Pyrland Road
Newington Green
London, N.
28th Nov., 1884

Rev. W. T. Storrs
Dear Sir,

Mr. D. E. Hoste of Brighton has applied to us desiring to labor as a missionary in China, and has referred us to you for a testimonial to his character.

As it is most desirable that the greatest care be taken in the selection of candidates for missionary work, we should feel greatly obliged if you would kindly reply to the appended inquiries regarding the applicant, in so far as you feel warranted in doing so.

I am, dear Sir,
Yours truly,
B. Broomhall, Sec.

Mr. Storrs read through the questions. He duly considered what he knew of the young Artillery officer, and then filled in the form.

Q. How long have you known the applicant?
A. About two years.
Q. How long, to your knowledge, has he been a professing Christian?
A. Soon after I knew him.
Q. What opinions have you formed of his Christian character?
A. Very high. A simple, straightforward fellow, with much love and faith.
Q. Knowledge of Scripture?
A. Fair. But he is a young Christian.
Q. Doctrinal views?
A. On all important points quite clear.

Q. Do you consider he possesses the following requisites for a missionary?
1. Genuine love for souls, leading to earnest efforts for their salvation?
A. Most certainly, but he is naturally rather shy.
2. Sound judgment and common sense?
A. A little impulsive perhaps, but a clear head.
3. Ability to learn?
A. He must have some ability, or he could not have got his commission in the Artillery.
4. Ability to teach?
A. I cannot say. I should not think he has much.
5. A patient, persevering disposition?
A. Cannot say. I think he ought to have persevered in the calling wherein he was called.
6. A fair amount of energy and enterprise?
A. I should hope so; but I do not think he is naturally enterprising.
7. Good health and average physical strength?
A. Certainly.
Q. Has he, to your knowledge, been engaged in any kind of evangelistic work?
A. He tried to do a little while resident here.
Q. If so, of what nature?
A. Open-air preaching. I was not present, but heard that he did fairly well.
Q. How long engaged in it?
A. Not long – only once or twice to my knowledge.
Q. How has he acquitted himself in it?
A. Fairly – so I heard.
Q. If you know any particulars which, in your opinion, would on the one hand specially qualify him for missionary work, or, on the other hand, hinder his usefulness as a missionary, will you kindly state them?
A. When I heard that he had offered himself as a missionary I was sorry, for I did not think he was naturally fitted for such work; but I may be mistaken. My sympathy with mission work is so great that I

did not grudge him, but I should have liked him to have remained in the Army and worked among the men. Your mission has my constant prayers – though I am an old C.M.S. man, I never forget the China Inland Mission in my special intercessions.
(Signature)   W. T. STORRS.
(Address)   Sandown Vicarage, Isle of Wight.

It was not a particularly promising testimonial to the suitability of the applicant! "Not naturally enterprising.... Naturally rather shy.... Not naturally suited for missionary work." It would not have been surprising if the mission authorities had decided that he was not the type of man required for the task of evangelizing inland China. He was hampered by a curiously high-pitched voice from being an impressive public speaker; his reserved temperament prevented him from making easy contacts; even his personal appearance was against his making a favorable first impression on the Chinese, who would look with suspicion on a "foreign devil" with light blue eyes and hair of a ginger hue!

The spiritual stature of the quiet young man had not passed unnoticed by the experienced workers at Pyrland Road, however. His humility and sincerity were evident, and even in those early days his balanced judgment and foresight were appreciated by those who knew him. Of his willingness for self-sacrifice there could be no doubt, for it was no small matter for an Army officer of good family to renounce what promised to be a distinguished career in order to join a poor and little-known mission whose members were expected to "bury themselves" in the interior of China; and his ability to endure physical hardship and privation was fairly assured by the doctor's report that, though he was not strong, he was healthy. He seemed to possess qualities that would endure, spiritually, mentally, and physically, and he himself was now sufficiently convinced of God's will to resign his commission. He was therefore accepted as a probationer before the year ended.

From that time events moved rapidly. In those days there was not the prolonged period of training for candidates which was later seen to be necessary. Six other young men, including two or three with whom he had already been intimately connected in a mutual desire to carry the good news of salvation to China, had also been accepted by the mission, and on February 4th, 1885, the seven of them arrived at one of the largest halls in London to take part in their final valedictory meeting before setting sail.

It was a time when the rising tide of a spiritual revival was quickening the Christian world, with the result that a great impetus was given to foreign mission enterprise. There was a whole-hearted response to the challenge of heathendom on the part of believers in many different walks of life, and it was no very unusual sight to see young men and women leaving home and loved ones, renouncing much that life holds dear, in order to go and preach Christ among the heathen. Nevertheless, the meeting in Exeter Hall that evening was not an ordinary one. Much attention had been drawn to the new missionary recruits, some of whom were well-known in the sporting world, and whose names were household words. Two of them had just completed an evangelistic tour of England and Scotland, in which many people had professed conversion; while all of them were of sufficiently good birth and position to excite some curiosity.

In spite, therefore, of pouring rain, the hall was so densely packed that, to quote a current report, "it appeared to be a living mass of human beings," while an overflow meeting had to be held elsewhere. On the platform, besides prominent Christian leaders of the day, were forty undergraduates from Cambridge, who had come specially to wish God-speed to the seven young men who were to set sail for China on the morrow.

What a hush of expectancy as these young men, five graduates from Cambridge and two Army officers, take their places on the platform! One by one, with varying degrees of eloquence, but uniform sincerity, they speak. Here is C. T. Studd, who two years previously was captain of the Cambridge University Cricket Eleven; Stanley Smith, stroke of the Cambridge Eight in 1882; Montagu Beauchamp, nephew of Lord Radstock; Arthur Polhill-Turner, and his brother Cecil, an officer in the Dragoon

Guards; the Rev. W. W. Cassels; and D. E. Hoste, an officer in the Artillery. His short address lacks the winsome eloquence of Smith, the burning earnestness of Studd, the picturesque challenge of Cassels. Standing there for the first and last time in his life, as he supposes, to address an audience of that size, he is grateful for the opportunity to ask for the prayers of so many. After giving his testimony in a few concise sentences, he expresses his thanks to God for the prayers that have already gone up on their behalf and asks for a continuance of them. And as he resumes his seat, who can foretell that this one of the seven is to be for thirty-five years the leader of the Mission they are just entering? Yet the quiet influence of his unselfconscious godliness made its impression even then. Amy Carmichael, founder of the Dohnavur Fellowship of South India, saw a report of that meeting in the first missionary book she ever read. "Specially I was drawn in spirit," she writes, "to one who had counted loss all that life as an officer of the Royal Artillery would have meant, and who had become a corn of wheat, willing to fall into the ground and die."

One last intimate glimpse is vouchsafed of him before he left England. There are few more poignant moments in a missionary's life than those in which he bids farewell to his own people and turns his face towards a strange land. There is a keen edge on that sacrifice which cuts to depths untouched before and leaves an indelible impression on the memory. Sixty years later, one of D. E. Hoste's brothers wrote:

"I remember the moment of his leaving our home at Brighton very clearly. We were nearly all of us at home for the occasion. The cab was at the door. There was a short commendatory prayer, a few last words with my mother, a warm embrace, and he was gone to his life work.

"From time to time he has been back amongst us since that distant day, but always as a visitor. His ticket on that occasion may be said to have been a single one, and the China to which he traveled then as a stranger and a newcomer was henceforth his home."

Chapter 3

First Impressions

On the day following the great valedictory meeting, the seven young men set out for China. Across the continent to Brindisi, by steamer to Alexandria, by train to Suez, where they embarked for Colombo, and finally on to Shanghai, they traveled, sounding out the gospel as they went. An independent observer wrote: "On their arrival at Suez many wondered what they would be like; surely there must be something wrong, a screw loose somewhere, that seven young men of position should leave home and all the pleasures of a fashionable life – to convert Chinamen! We expected no end of fun in quizzing them." But instead of indulging in polite if contemptuous banter at the expense of the missionaries as they started to sing, the passengers who gathered round found themselves listening in a hush which somehow they did not care to break. There was a simplicity and earnestness about these young men which forbad jesting, and a conviction about their preaching which could not be gainsaid. The "Cambridge Seven," as they came to be called, were in the full stream of a spiritual revival, and many were the prayers that ascended to God on their behalf from the home country. It is not to be wondered at, therefore, that their words came with power to the hearts of their listeners.

Stanley Smith and C. T. Studd were perhaps the outstanding members of the group. Their fame in the world of sport would alone have been sufficient to attract attention, but both were gifted speakers as well. Montagu Beauchamp's forceful enthusiasm could not pass unnoticed, while W. W. Cassels had a genial charm which drew people to him. Amongst these more striking personalities, the quiet young Artillery officer moved unobtrusively, witnessing in his own way. He was rarely the one to speak at the big meetings arranged on board ship or at the different ports of call; but it was he who first established contact with one of their fellow passengers, the blasphemous, drunken captain of an Indian steamer, whose subsequent conversion was recorded as being "a great and notable miracle." This man had already made up his mind he would have some fun at the expense of the seven young missionaries who were to come aboard at Suez. D. E. Hoste, quite unconscious of the life and character of the man, got into conversation with him almost immediately. The captain asserted that he considered the Bible "all rot," and did not believe it or understand it. It was, therefore, the more surprising that he consented to read it with his new acquaintance, who advised him to "pray God to help him, and persevere!" For three or four days the two spent many hours together, reading and discussing the whole of John's Gospel and a large part of Romans. The captain's attitude changed considerably; and one day, after a long conversation with C. T. Studd, he went to his cabin and received the Lord Jesus Christ as his Savior.

"The next day Hoste spoke to him," wrote C. T. Studd in a long letter describing the whole affair, "and was overjoyed to find him rejoicing in the knowledge of his salvation, and they had prayer together.

"I can tell you it was a treat to hear him at our afternoon prayer meeting, the way he just poured out his heart to God in thanksgiving for his wonderful love, and pleaded for the salvation of those on board; he seemed to be a full-grown Christian all at once, and boldly testified almost every night before the ship's company of what the Lord Jesus had done for him and the peace and joy he was experiencing. It was delightful to hear him say, 'You know it's so simple; it's just trusting, simply trusting.'

"You can well imagine that there was no small stir in the ship. Previous to our coming on board, the refrigerator man had said, 'Well, if the captain is converted, then I will begin to think seriously of religion.' There was an increasing interest in the meetings; several of the stewards and of the crew were converted;

two backsliders were restored, and all the second class passengers were converted."

It was not only on board that the quiet witnessing went on, however. D. E. Hoste could not forget that he had been in the Army, and at the various ports of call the garrisons seemed to draw him.

"At Alexandria," he wrote, "we were able to give some tracts at the barracks for our men."

Cecil Polhill-Turner, the other ex-Army officer in the group, reported from Penang: "Hoste and I, with a Dr. Macklin, went up to the barracks, where there were two companies of the 27th Regiment.... After giving away some books and having some personal conversations, we walked quickly back to the landing-stage."

At Singapore, too, the barracks were visited, and a number of soldiers came in the evening to the meeting held in the town hall, while at Hong Kong, where several meetings were arranged for the "Cambridge Seven," many soldiers were in the audiences.

All the time, the life of prayer that increasingly characterized Hoste was being cultivated. Writing of the conversion of a young planter on his way to India, he gave an unconscious insight into his own spiritual life!

"The following, among others, is an instance of the Lord's working. It was in the case of a young fellow, a Dane, going out as a planter to India. One of our party had been led to have two talks with him on the subject of his soul's salvation, and then for several days scarcely any other opportunity offered for further conversation. As he could only speak a little broken English, and did not understand it well, it was difficult to know how far the words had affected him. However, one night he came up to one of us at about 10 p.m. and said he wished to come to Jesus, and soon found peace and joy in believing. Some of us had been watching in prayer for him, and had observed that for two or three days previous he had been very quiet and silent, so we were not surprised."

Watching in prayer, he observed. It became his habitual attitude.

On March 18th the party reached their destination. On the quayside to greet them, unrecognized at first because of being dressed as a Chinese, was Hudson Taylor; and it was he who escorted them through the streets of Shanghai to the headquarters of the Mission. A good deal of interest had been created among the foreign community in Shanghai in the "Cambridge Seven," and special meetings were arranged for them before they started inland to the distant province of Shansi, where they were to begin their lives as missionaries. Not only those who were friendly towards missions attended the meetings, but some who were definitely opposed to the gospel; and once more the young men had the joy of seeing souls converted to God. As in other places, the principal speakers were C. T. Studd and Stanley Smith; and D. E. Hoste attracted far less attention than some of the other members of the group. One who was in Shanghai at the time, however, observed: "Those who saw more of him were impressed by his lowliness."

The meetings over, it was time for the young men to start on their journey inland. Western clothes must be discarded and strange, loose-fitting Chinese garments donned instead. Manners would need to be altered. The brisk, quick step of healthy youth must be slowed down to the leisurely stroll of the Oriental; a strict watch kept over every gesture and every word, lest some careless movement or a raised voice give offense and the gospel thereby be hindered. And they must start to grow their hair that they, too, could have the long queues worn by Chinese men in that period. "I am made all things to all men," said the apostle Paul, "that by all means I may save some." For this same reason the missionaries had to conform to Chinese clothes and manners rather than Western. It was decided that the party should divide, and travel by different routes to Shansi. D. E. Hoste, Stanley Smith and W. W. Cassels, with F. W. Baller as escort, were to travel via Tientsin and Peking; and it was in the picturesque old capital of China that they saw the greatest response to their ministry. Meetings had been arranged for them amongst the small English community, and to their great joy a number of their own fellow countrymen were converted.

"But the remarkable work," wrote W. W. Cassels, "has been at the afternoon gatherings, chiefly of missionaries and their families, for prayer and the deepening of spiritual life. Dear Stanley has conducted these with great power, and with most manifest help from on high."

"He began to speak about the comparatively small result of missionary work, of the acknowledged failure and want of power of the great mass of missionaries, and he has been going on to show how vast are the promises of God, and that they are almost all conditional upon the outpouring of the Spirit of God, and we have been exhorted to cry to him mightily and to wait upon him with a persevering faith until the Spirit be poured out upon us from on high. As a result, we are pressed to delay our departure over this last Sunday, and now the missionaries meet together for two hours every afternoon for prayer and for further exhortation. Each day God has been working."

So great was the impression made that an appeal for united prayer was sent out to missionaries in other parts of China, signed by twenty-five missionaries representing four different societies in Peking.

The chief speaker, as always, was Stanley Smith; and D. E. Hoste was again a quiet, prayerful spectator in the background. He had no special gift for public speaking. Yet it was on this journey up to Shansi that a different gift, which was late to have so important a place in his service, was observed. He little thought, when he wrote a letter of thanks to the hostess who had entertained him in Tientsin, that it would ever reach the leaders of the Mission. She was so impressed by it, however, that she showed it to J. W. Stevenson, Hudson Taylor's deputy; and years later that man, who must have read thousands of letters, still remembered it. The deep thinker, whose high-pitched voice and restrained manner prevented him from ever swaying large audiences, could express himself, when he took his pen in his hand, with a grace and clarity which few could equal.

In the district of Southern Shansi to which the new missionaries were sent a remarkable work of God had already commenced. Some years previously a confirmed opium smoker named Hsi had been converted, and became an outstanding witness to the power of the gospel. His whole life was transformed. He spent hours, sometimes days, in prayer, and his preaching was in the power of the Holy Spirit. Saved himself from the lust for opium, he knew that others could be delivered likewise. At that time, it was said that in the province of Shansi "eleven out of every ten" smoked opium, and the country was fast being reduced to poverty as a result. In addition to the evangelistic and pastoral work in which he was voluntarily engaged, Hsi had already opened several opium refuges, to which came men and women desiring to break off the terrible habit. Here they received the medicine that Hsi himself compounded from recipes which had come quite simply to his mind after a period of fasting and prayer. Not only did they receive medicine, however, but they also heard the gospel message. Only through faith in the risen Savior, and prayer offered in his all-prevailing name, could they be permanently delivered from the terrible habit which gripped them like a vice. The voice of importunate prayer was constantly heard, often by night as well as by day, in Hsi's refuges; and many were the drug addicts who were delivered from its power.

Largely as a result of this man's work and witness, there were now little groups of believers, numbering about 100 baptized church members in all, scattered over the Pingyang plain, an area of about twenty-five miles broad and sixty miles wide. It was in this district that four of the "Cambridge Seven" were to commence their missionary life.

For a few weeks they lived together in Pingyang, a very happy party, working hard at language study all day and enjoying their walks around the city walls in the evening. Looking over the city, they saw the crowded streets and watched with interest the water carriers, the street vendors, the dignified officials in their long silk gowns – the human beings to whom they longed to tell the glad tidings of a Savior from sin; while across the plain they saw the not distant mountains lit up by the setting sun. Daily they met together for prayer and praise and the study of God's Word, rejoicing in that peculiar sense of privilege experienced by those who have been separated unto the gospel.

It was, however, in conditions of even greater separation from the delights of Western civilization and congenial companionship that D. E. Hoste entered into a deeper spiritual experience. In July he was sent, with Mr. Key, another young missionary, and a Chinese evangelist, to Küwu, a small city about fifty miles south of Pingyang. The district had suffered much from a recent famine, the sad traces of which still remained. Villages were more than half-depopulated, houses broken down, walls crumbling, roads and bridges unrepaired. For about eight months he lived here, his days mostly spent in language study, to which he diligently applied himself. Mails were few and far between, and sometimes weeks passed without any arriving. One day, after such a period, a mail arrived, and his first impulse was, of course, to sit down and read his letters. He was arrested by the thought, however, that had he been still in the Army he would not thus have allowed the personal to take first place. Why should he be more lax in serving as a missionary? Resolutely putting away his letters until lunch time, he resumed his study.

After a day of language study, Hoste and Key often spent the evening sitting out in the courtyard of the rented house, with some fifteen or twenty young Chinese squatting on the ground around, drawn by their interest in the two missionaries, yet willing to listen quietly as Chang, the evangelist, preached to them. During their daily walk, late in the afternoon, the young men distributed tracts in the city and the surrounding villages; and later on, when they had gained sufficient knowledge of the language to "speak out intelligibly the facts of the gospel," they visited some of the fairs held in the market towns and villages of their district, where they had good opportunities for preaching and tract distribution.

In the midst of this full and busy life, the young missionary's mind was continually occupied with the consciousness of an inner conflict. Well he knew that his sins were forgiven. Well he knew that he was the possessor of a new life, the life of God himself implanted within. Yet he felt another life beside the divine one operating in his inmost being, harassing him with disturbing thoughts and emotions.

> *This cruel self, oh, how it strives,*
> *And works within my breast,*
> *To come between Thee and my soul*
> *And keep me back from rest!*

That he longed to overcome the inward foe there can be no doubt. Hudson Taylor, in a letter to his wife written in the summer of that year, said: "I fear both S. Smith and Hoste have injured themselves by over-fasting." In the case of D. E. Hoste, at any rate, it seems that the root cause of his intense zeal and concern was not so much for others as for himself. His earnest desire for deliverance did not continue long unsatisfied.

It was largely through the reading of *Luther on Galatians*, combined with his regular Bible study, that the way of deliverance was gradually made plain.

"I have been blessed in seeing more clearly the simplicity of the gospel," he wrote. "How that it is at the Cross we find deliverance from sin and self, and not in prayings and strugglings. The words, '*Ye are dead*, and your life is hidden with Christ in God' and 'Reckon yourselves *dead*' were brought home to me. I have always been trying, by much prayer and diligence, to make the flesh dead, with painful results of failure; not daring to say, 'I *am* dead,' on the authority of God's Word, independent of all the tusslings of the flesh. It came to me that God's order was just by faith to take hold of his covenant as I was in all the depths of helplessness, and by faith to believe that I have been crucified with Christ, and that Christ lives in me, not as the result of any tremendous devotion or effort on my part, but in sheer grace, because God has chosen to deal with me thus. What a glorious gospel for poor hopeless, helpless ones! I never was naturally much of a man for shouting as a way of expressing my feelings, but when this wonderful love of God in Christ comes before me, I feel I must shout, 'Hallelujah! Glory to God and the Lamb!' The old habits of unbelief and restlessness, and giving way to feelings, have attacked me tremendously, but by God's grace I have been enabled to keep hold of the simple word, *'Ye are dead,'* etc. I see the battle is just by faith to keep the position which God has given in Christ."

A further insight into his spiritual life and growth during the next few months is given in the letters he wrote to Hudson Taylor. These were mainly concerned with respectful but friendly reports of his activities and the progress of the work. Now and then, however, a more intimate note would creep in, revealing his true humility of spirit and the source and motive power of his life and service.

> Küwu, Shansi
> Dec. 9th, 1885
>
> I have settled not to give food to these men who come to enquire about the gospel. (There was wisdom in this decision. Too often a promising work has been spoiled at the outset by a missionary, with the best of intentions, providing pecuniary and material help where it was really not needed, thus encouraging "rice Christians.") At first sight it seems stingy, and I am quite open to a change as I get further light. I suppose we must be willing to learn by experience, though I should value your counsel, I need not say, very much, if you could kindly give it in a future letter. I have decided to eat my food with the evangelist, and in his way, of course; I have been doubtful on the matter, as he is in receipt of pay, but think that the principle of getting alongside of a man before trying to give him a leg up, which you brought before us so powerfully in our Bible readings in Shanghai, and in those papers in *China's Millions*, in short, the principle of the gospel leads me to it. I know there are reasons against it, but so there are against any

course. I would ask your prayers that God would give me some real unselfish love for these poor men or, rather, that I may so abide in Christ that his love for them may find expression in this mortal body."

Küwu, Shansi
2nd March, 1886

I would include myself, too, in my request for your prayers, and also that I may be helped with the language and get an entrance amongst these people. More and more I see that there will be need of much love and forbearance and willingness to be the inferior if one is really to get across the gulf there is between us. I do indeed praise God for having graciously allowed me to join in this fight out here. The Bible just becomes a new book in many parts, now one is in a position where one really is an alien and despised. It is a fellowship with the Lord Jesus which I knew not when in my native country. Only the other day, I was feeling rather tired and sore from little acts of rudeness and contempt, and the general atmosphere of total want of sympathy, which I doubt not you know and have experienced in a Chinese street. As I left the city, that hymn, "My Jesus, I love thee, I know thou art mine," just came like a sweet, warm echo from above; and as he seemed to shine upon me with his presence, I felt how blessed to have in any faint measure fellowship with him, and how loving of him, amidst all the affairs of heaven and earth, to turn aside, as it were, to minister to one poor, weak sheep! Oh, for more of his Spirit, to be willing to help another, to be quick to see when another needs help.

A good deal of his time was spent alone, as his fellow missionary went to other districts. In order to free his servant to cook for the men in the opium refuge, and also to save housekeeping, which as he naively put it, "I never was good at," he usually took his meals at a nearby food shop. It is not surprising, therefore, that the strain of this unaccustomed life told on his highly-strung system; and when he returned to Pingyang for the Spring Conference in 1886, he was not at all well.

He wrote:

"In weariness often" is something you must know about, dear Mr. Taylor. I remember so well your address at the Mildmay Conference of 1884, on the "Knowledge of God," and oh! how glad we shall be for everything which brought us really into fellowship with him, down here. The remembrance of your great toils and labors often comes to me when tempted to give way to weariness or discouragement, and I just feel ashamed of myself."

With physical weakness came a tendency to despondency.

Thank you for your words of exhortation and warning lest I become slack about the souls of these men. How deeply I need them! How little of any real, unselfish love for their souls, how little of Christ – I feel it deeply. Of course, in oneself, absolutely devoid of any true love – and yet how one ought to be animated by the new and divine life! And as you say, it is our portion to be channels for that life to flow through, "except unbelief hinder." Oh, that one knew really deeply those words, "Not I, but Christ." Alas! How often I feel it reversed in me. But as Studd says, we want to keep praising and never mind ourselves; or else I find I get most hopelessly into the dumps. Will you ask that I may really know what it is to walk *before God*, to be supremely tender and exercised as to his judgment of my life and service, and thus to be delivered from the fearful anxiety lest self should not receive its recognition and praise from my fellow men.

He spent most of the summer in Pingyang, where greater privacy on the compound afforded better opportunity for the rest he was needing, and also for the study of the written language. More important even than language was the practical out-working of the love for souls implanted in his heart, however. With returning physical strength came the urge to go out amongst the people and make known to them the gospel with which he had been entrusted. To witness for Christ is rarely an easy thing, especially for those who are naturally reserved. It must have cost the young Artillery officer much self-humbling to preach in the open air by the sea in England, where fellow officers and men could see and hear and where he would often observe the surprised amusement of passers-by. As a missionary in far-away China it was no easier to stand in a crowded street, exposed to the open curiosity and often contempt of the men and women of another race, and proclaim in halting words a message which was as a strange, fantastic story to most who listened. Yet, like Paul of old, necessity was laid upon him. Harder to be endured than the scorn of man would be the inner heaviness and darkness of spirit that comes to those who fail to confess their Savior before others. He found that a love for souls prospered and grew as he saw the need of those without Christ, and, seeing, proclaimed the provision already made to meet it. The Chinese language must be mastered, and most of his time and strength were given to that. Time must also be given for the prayer without which life and service become fruitless. But even that was not sufficient. In August we find him writing:

"I purpose, by God's help, to preach daily on the streets at 5:30 p.m. I feel that three months on end without any contact with the mass of beloved fellow men outside would be enough to stifle any faint love I may have, through God's grace. 'Out of sight, out of mind' is, I have found, true...."

Chapter 4

Hungtung

"The one thing the work needs is a head or captain – not too strong on the one hand, nor a weakling on the other – who would unite in one all the branches of work. Everything seems loose, and consequently feeble."

It was during the summer of 1886 that Hudson Taylor visited South Shansi, and that was his summing-up of the situation regarding C.I.M. work in the district. Much had been accomplished in the ten years since the province was first entered. The great famine of 1877-8 had provided an opportunity for widespread relief work on the part of missionaries, and their whole-hearted and self-sacrificing efforts to alleviate the suffering around them did much to quiet the suspicions with which they had previously been regarded. In the following years not a few souls were saved, among them men of strong character and with a real zeal for God's kingdom, Hsi being the most outstanding of them all. Small groups of believers were being gathered out, willing and eager to be taught more of the power of their new-found Savior and how best they could follow him. With the lack of organized supervision, however, there was a danger of each group becoming an isolated unit rather than a member of the living, growing body. Hudson Taylor saw the need for someone to be invested with authority in the eyes of the local Christians, and it seemed evident that the man already appointed of God for this position was Hsi. Throughout the whole district he was known and loved by the Christians, many of whom were his own spiritual children. It was largely through his opium refuge work that little churches were being established. What more fitting than that he should be openly acknowledged, by missionary and Chinese alike, as one called and appointed by God for a widespread pastoral ministry?

At first Hsi, realizing the additional responsibility that the position of ordained pastor would involve, and deeply conscious of his own inadequacy, was unwilling to accept it. He was eventually persuaded that it was the Lord's will, however; and, once convinced on that point, he refused no longer.

The solemn ordination service, when Hudson Taylor laid hands upon the man kneeling before him, separating him to "watch over and feed the church of God," marked an epoch in the work in Shansi. It was the first time a Chinese had been ordained there and appointed to a position approximating that of a bishop. It involved a subtle change in the relationship between the Mission and the little Chinese churches that had been brought into being, and a readjustment in the attitude of the missionaries to the newly-appointed church leader. The building of an indigenous church, which was Hudson Taylor's aim, might well have been seriously hindered had not the right type of missionary worked with Hsi. With all his gifts and spiritual power, he was known to be extremely strong-willed and not always an easy man with whom to cooperate. By their very newness to the situation, and consequent freedom from preconceived ideas about the man, the young missionaries who worked in his district were probably better qualified to be closely associated with him than might have been older ones. They realized their own inexperience in church oversight, even in the homeland, while their short period in China and limited knowledge of the language and the customs prevented them from interfering in matters when the temptation to "put things right" might otherwise have proved too strong!

It was with Stanley Smith that Hsi first became intimate. He had early been attracted by the young man's sunny nature, willingness to give himself in service for others, and evident spiritual power, and desiring to open an opium refuge in Hungtung had enlisted his help and cooperation. The Mission's approval of the suggestion having been obtained, premises were eventually secured in the city, the refuge was opened, and Stanley Smith was installed. This was in May, 1886.

In the autumn of that year D. E. Hoste joined him – not without an inward conflict. Only after a number of years had passed did he refer publicly to the struggle he had had before going to the station in which he afterwards labored for about ten years.

Although Pastor Hsi was praying that Hoste might go to Hungtung, it was Stanley Smith who invited him to do so. In making the proposal, Smith proceeded to say that, when decisions were to be made, it would be necessary that one of them should be in the position of leader, and decide matters. Not unnaturally, having already been in Hungtung for some time, and being on terms of close fellowship with Hsi, the Chinese leader, he felt himself better qualified than Hoste to fill this position, and therefore planned to do so.

"When he put the matter thus bluntly to me, I was ruffled in my spirit," admitted D. E. Hoste at a meeting he was addressing many years later. "Why should I serve under him? We were about the same age, and had come to China together. Granted he was brilliant with the language, could make easy contacts, and in other ways was my superior, this did not seem sufficient reason to me, so I suggested he should write to the Mission at Shanghai for a younger man, as it was their business to make appointments.

"Later, on thinking over the situation, the Spirit of God probed me, and I was forced to admit that I did not relish the thought of being under my friend. I thought of my 'face,' what friends would surmise, etc. The difficulty was in my own heart. It was impressed upon me that unwillingness persisted in would mean my having to part company with the Lord Jesus Christ, who dwells with the humble ones, those who willingly go down. I therefore accepted my friend's suggestion, and we worked happily together for several months....

"Pride and self-will are hateful in the sight of God. They are indeed referred to by the Scriptures as in a particular sense characteristic of Satan himself. It is a solemn fact that they may be exhibited equally in the exercise of oversight and in opposition thereto.

"We see God's character in the Lamb of God. He was brought as a lamb to the slaughter and he opened not his mouth. Even in exaltation in heaven he is depicted as 'a lamb as it had been slain.' That is his character. He is perfectly humble. When we are tempted to exalt self and resent being put down or overlooked, we need to beware. Satan said, 'I will be like the most High.' Pride and ambition are essentially Satanic characteristics. Everything that savors of self-exaltation is kith and kin to Satan.

"The Lord thus, in a practical way, taught me this truth. I believe that crises like these, when we are tested as to our willingness to go down, are the pivotal influences that shape our destiny. Our subsequent ministry springs from the decisions we make in these critical places." The man who was to become a spiritual leader must needs learn the secret of that submission which God can trust with exaltation.

D. E. Hoste therefore went to Hungtung and deliberately took the place of junior under Stanley Smith. They lived just as the Chinese around them – not always an easy thing for the Westerner to do. It is not only a matter of eating Chinese food, wearing Chinese clothes, living in Chinese houses. More trying than this to the Englishman "whose home is his castle" is the unaccustomed publicity in which he must be prepared to live. The Chinese know little of privacy, and closed doors are practically unknown, except at night! Meals are eaten more or less publicly, and visitors wander into courtyards, interrupting reading, working, or any other employment, without hesitation. The missionary who shuts his front door during the daytime and refuses to see visitors is liable to be regarded with suspicion as to his occupation and motive in coming to China.

An insight into the lives of the two young missionaries is given in a letter written from Hungtung by D. E. Hoste:

> We have the custom here of an open door at all times, so that study is liable to be interrupted. Our dinner hour is the

time, however! We generally have squads of six or eight, who sit on forms and watch us eat, carrying on conversation freely. There is no doubt it pays; though until one definitely takes it as in the commission, it is apt at times to be exasperating to have one's meal interrupted to give a lesson in geography to someone who wants to have the mysteries of one of Mr. Stanley Smith's maps explained to him. It gives grand opportunities for preaching the gospel, and then a hymn or two, accompanied on the harmonium, fairly sweeps away any lingering prejudice against us, apparently.

The young men spent most of their time, however, in the country. Dividing the country churches into sections, they arranged circuits, visiting between fifteen and twenty little centers regularly, teaching the new converts and preaching to enquirers. The ground had been well prepared by Pastor Hsi's faithful and energetic service, and everywhere they went they found a real readiness to hear the Word of God.

Stanley Smith, particularly, seemed invested with spiritual power in an unusual measure. Speaking of him many years later, D. E. Hoste said, "He was full of the Spirit. I shall never forget those months I lived with him in Hungtung. There was such a lot of prayer going up for him; so many people at home had been impressed with him and were praying for him. God used that man. The more he was willing to let Pastor Hsi keep his natural position, the more God seemed to bless him. The power that came down was really very great. The Spirit of God seemed sometimes just to fill the place when he was preaching."

The six months of intensive country work culminated in a convention held in Hungtung in the spring of 1887, the like of which had probably never been seen in China. For two days beforehand Pastor Hsi, with characteristic intensity, gave himself to prayer and fasting. The necessary arrangements for providing food and accommodation for about 300 people were carried out with unusual ease and smoothness. Meanwhile, from the country districts around came the little groups of men and women who so recently had turned to God from idols, eager for Christian fellowship and the opportunity for meeting together to hear the Words of life for which they were so hungry. It was at this convention that the largest number of people in the history of the Mission to be baptized in one day took the step which separated them openly from the heathen around as being disciples of Jesus Christ.

When it was known that 216 people had been baptized in Hungtung, the news was received with delight in England, but with some apprehension on the part of missionaries in China. Such a "mass movement" was hitherto unknown. Could it really be that all those who became church members that day were truly converted? In the days to come Pastor Hsi and the two missionaries were severely criticized by some for their action. Not all who were baptized on that occasion continued to bear a good testimony, and in later years Pastor Hsi and D. E. Hoste agreed that it was necessary to exercise greater care in accepting enquirers for baptism. While some failed, however, the vast majority of those baptized stood firm. Five years later it was reported that of the 216 baptized, seven were transferred to other churches, four had died, fifty had definitely backslid, while another twenty were difficult to trace. Of the backsliders, most of whom returned to opium smoking, less than twenty lapsed into idolatry, while some still continued to hold family worship. One hundred and thirty-five remained faithful. There can be little doubt that the convention was a high water-mark of spiritual blessing in the district of South Shansi.

A few days after the convention the two missionaries set out for a journey up to Taiyüan, where they planned to spend the summer months in concentrating on language study. Leaving the district in which the gospel was being widely preached, and where they had seen a spiritual harvest that had filled them with joy, they were brought face to face again with a great block of heathendom, where was not a single witness for Christ. Compared with the hundreds of thousands of people living on the plain through which they now traveled, who were passing on towards eternity without ever even hearing the only name given whereby men can be saved, how small a number seemed the two hundred-odd over whom they had been rejoicing! With the incomparable sense of privilege to be telling the good news of free salvation to those who had never heard came a consciousness of the inadequacy of the witness. On reaching the capital of the province, D. E. Hoste wrote:

> As we passed up the plain we had grand times of tract distributing and preaching; but oh, what a mockery it seemed to tell a poor fellow who asked about breaking off opium, that there was no place nearer than 160 to 200 *li!*
>
> We found willing listeners everywhere; but how one's heart ached as we felt there was not a single man who was caring for these souls, and then thought of streets at home with churches, chapels, mission halls, meeting houses, coffee houses, and institutions of all kinds; while here positively not a single room in which a work was going on in whole cities. May God rouse the church at home further, and make them remember the masses. It is just awful!
>
> May a gracious God fit one for his service! How he must be longing for anybody whom he can pick up to satisfy his great heart of love in gathering in multitudes of the lost. One feels one has scarcely got a glimmer of John 3:16: "God so loved the world." What an infinitely solemn and important matter God must have regarded the salvation of souls as being – he gave up his only Son! And one catches oneself doubting whether one can give up some little comfort for the same object!

Not as much time was given to language study as had at first been planned. In Taiyüan also innumerable opportunities presented themselves for proclaiming the gospel, and how could they shut themselves into their studies when in the soldiers' camps, among the patients in the mission hospital, and on the streets were people willing to listen to the Word of life? In August, when the rains came, and street preaching was therefore curtailed, they moved up to the hills, intending to apply themselves more diligently to their book work.

Meanwhile, things were not going well in Hungtung. Some of Pastor Hsi's colleagues in the opium refuge work, especially one named Fan, who had for some time been resentful of his increasing power and authority, suddenly turned against him. Accusing him of currying favor with the foreigners for his own financial advancement, they deliberately employed men to slander the reputation of the refuge work; and they themselves set up opposition refuges, underselling Hsi while using his own prescriptions. The Hungtung church, with its large numbers of new believers, was soon divided against itself, part remaining loyal to Hsi, part swayed by the vitriolic fury of Fan and his adherents. Added to the troubles in Hungtung there were unexpected disasters in some of the more distant refuges, where the death of some patients involved Hsi in much perplexity and distress of mind. It seemed that the principalities and powers of darkness against whom he was conscious of fighting had planned an offensive that threatened to wreck his whole work.

Even before leaving Hungtung, Stanley Smith had felt the urge to commence work in Luan, a city seventy or eighty miles east of Pingyang; and after the summer he soon proceeded to take up his new field of service. D. E. Hoste, therefore, returned alone to stand with Pastor Hsi in his dark hour.

What a different state of affairs he found in Hungtung to that which he had left behind! The church that had been progressing so rapidly was weakened by division, while the refuge work which had been such a testimony to the power of God seemed in danger of being overthrown.

It was a critical time indeed. There were those even amongst the missionaries who doubted the wisdom of all Hsi's methods, and who felt that the attack against him might not have been without provocation. D. E. Hoste himself was by no means blind to the faults of the Chinese leader. "He was a man who was impatient, and had a quick temper, and a defect in his character was this: he was apt to be suspicious. He was very slow to give himself away to anybody."

Was it because he recognized the same tendency in himself that the ex-Artillery officer understood the Confucian scholar better probably than anyone else ever had? Was it because he, too, was very slow to give himself away to anybody that he did not wonder that he must first *prove himself worthy of trust* before Hsi would trust him?

The seriousness of the situation was his opportunity. Hsi's own colleagues, who had seemed faithful, had failed him. To whom else but the missionary could he now turn? For all his spiritual power, Hsi was but human, and this was one of the times when he needed the strengthening and sympathy of a fellow creature. In the furnace of one of the biggest trials of his life, Hsi found the young and inexperienced Englishman to be a friend who proved faithful; one who never tried to rule, but whose aim it was to be "guide, philosopher, and friend," as he himself said.

One of the first matters that concerned them both was the attitude they should adopt towards those who were slandering the refuge work and sowing seeds of dissension in the church. Should they take drastic action, separating the wheat from the tares, as it were? There seemed much to be said for taking such a course. Would it not hinder the poison from spreading farther? Would it not purify the church? But as they prayed they became more and more convinced that this was not the best way. The exercise of authority on the part of Hsi would only give Fan and his followers an opportunity for gaining further sympathy in their assertion of the Pastor's high handedness and arbitrary spirit. It was decided, therefore, to go on quietly, without any retaliation, and leave God to make manifest who were in the right. Hsi continued the supervision of his opium refuges and pastoral work, while D. E. Hoste acted as missionary in charge of the station of Hungtung.

It was not easy for him to avoid being drawn into unprofitable discussions with those who desired to bring Hsi into disrepute with the missionaries. On one occasion, when twenty or so of them took possession of the refuge at Hungtung, it was with a fast-beating heart that he knelt to pray before going in amongst the group of angry men to listen patiently to their accusations and reason with them. Visits to the little outstations connected with the central church provided welcome opportunities for getting away from the scene of so much strife.

"My journey around the Chaocheng and Fenhsi districts," he wrote, "was a time of real refreshment and rest. I do relish the exercise of walking over the hills in the lovely spring air, and then the kindly, respectful welcome and homely service and chat over God's Word is a delightful change from the friction of unreasonable and intractable dear fellows who beset one so at times when in Hungtung, with grievances and schemes of their own for doing work, which are clearly frivolous and perverse."

The policy he and Pastor Hsi adopted with regard to Fan and his followers proved eventually to be the right one. After some months, there were signs of disintegration in the opposing party. Fan's true character became increasingly manifest, and some of the men who, sincere but mistaken, had followed him withdrew. Pastor Hsi, after a period of prayer and fasting, felt convinced that the final collapse of the rival refuges was close at hand, and spoke of it in all the leading centers. "If a man abides not in me, he is cast forth as a branch, and is withered" was the word particularly impressed on his mind.

"Rest quietly and wait," he said. "We do not need to fight in this battle. Within three months you will see the last of these spurious refuges brought to an end."

The prophecy was fulfilled. One by one Fan's refuges failed, his chief confederate left him, and within three months he had given up the whole thing. Hsi's refuge work, on the other hand, after the period of fierce testing through which it had passed, grew and increased, twenty-one more refuges being opened during the years following the persecution.

Chapter Five

Preparation of a Leader

At a period of missionary work in China when few had the vision of a church with Chinese rather than foreign leadership, D. E. Hoste saw that this was imperative if the church was to be indigenous. Towards the attainment of this ideal his mind was firmly set, and in Hungtung he was given the opportunity of putting into practice the principles of cooperation which were already well formulated in his mind. He had no intention of bringing in drastic reforms, of trying to force the native church into a foreign mold. He believed in letting it grow after its own order, as live things should. Far more necessary than mere outward forms of church order were that the members should increase in their knowledge of God and his laws. He realized that by reason of his Christian heritage and upbringing he had a contribution to make to the infant church in which God had placed him, and that the most effective way of making that contribution would be through the church leader.

"It was a cox that was wanted," he said once. "Pastor Hsi was perfectly well able to stroke the boat, and he had got plenty of men to pull behind him. What was wanted was a little man to sort of steer."

A great deal of patience and humility were required to work with a man of such a vivid and dominating personality as Hsi. The Chinese leader's quick temper was not mellowed in a day, and there must have been many times when the young missionary found it hard to exercise self-control. In some ways it would have been easier to strike out alone, building up his own work on his own lines, rather than cooperate with this strong-willed man whose outlook it was often difficult for the Englishman to understand. Had he done so, however, he would have missed what later proved to be the best training for his real life work. His friendship with Pastor Hsi, which deepened as the years passed, gave him an insight into the Chinese mind which he would probably never have gained in any other way; while the experience in dealing with difficulties and problems in the church life in Hungtung prepared him for dealing with similar difficulties and problems connected with the whole Mission and the churches brought into being through its agency.

The chief way of dealing with these difficulties was always by prayer, and he had unusual opportunities of seeing its efficacy as he worked with Hsi. On one occasion, two Chinese preachers who had quarreled seriously came to Pastor Hsi about their difference, each accusing the other and demanding his dismissal. Receiving them hospitably into his home, Hsi retired to his room, remaining there for two days without food.

"When a quarrel of this kind arises there is not much use talking," he said. "You have got to give yourself to prayer, because it is the work of wicked spirits. They are at the back of it, and we have got to wrestle with them, not with flesh and blood, by prayer and fasting." At the end of two days the Lord gave him the inward assurance that the victory was won, and he came out to see the men. After a few words about the necessity for the confession of personal sin, and the futility of throwing the blame on others, he started to tell them that the Lord had convicted him of the mistake he had made in ever putting the two of them to work together. He saw now that they were temperamentally unsuited, and that he should have prayed more about the matter before appointing their work. The two men were both completely melted, each confessing his own unchristian attitude and behavior, and with the tears rolling down their cheeks all three of them knelt together and were filled anew with the Holy Spirit.

In the matter of dealing with workers, both Hsi and D. E. Hoste saw increasingly the necessity of very careful handling. "Men who have done good work in years gone by may get into a wrong spirit; but you cannot deal with them summarily. If you take premature action, before God's time has come, you only aggravate the trouble." And so, in later years, D. E. Hoste's advice to young missionaries was, "Never lance an abscess before it's ripe!"

During the early days of missionary work in Hungtung there had been great emphasis placed on the necessity for spreading abroad the gospel, and a number of new converts had been encouraged to go out preaching. Weak in the faith, and very ignorant, they were not always consistent in their witness. They would have been more effective living their normal lives at home, and telling the gospel quietly to their friends. As case after case of sometimes distressing failures occurred, the missionary and the Chinese leader began to say to each other, "This thing is not of God."

"It is no good forcing people beyond their capacity; they will only go sprawl!" said D. E. Hoste. "We saw it was far better to wait and see the men themselves manifested, and then lead them out when they are really able for it. Then, when the time had come, we were led; we were always praying about this, praying to God to lead us on, and it became quite clear when the time had arrived and the brethren were ready for it."

The progress of the gospel in the district did not continue unchallenged. There were problems to be faced and solved, not only in the ordering of church affairs, but also in dealing with the matter of the persecution of Christians by their heathen neighbors. In the early days of his conversion, Hsi, inexperienced and lacking in understanding of the deeper principles of living by faith in God, had been quick to take up the cudgels on behalf of church members whose rights were infringed by angry or crafty heathen neighbors. He did not hesitate to claim help and redress for them from the mandarin, and on occasion even went to the capital of the province to interview the governor, setting on foot legal proceedings which resulted in the confusion of the adversaries. Thus poor Christians were shielded from many troubles by this man of position and unusual ability. It was noticed, however, that in each case where this help had been given the spiritual life of the little community flagged and failed. The natural desire to fight for those who were united by faith and love to the same Lord proved, after all, unprofitable. The decision not to retaliate himself in the Fan troubles was probably the first definite step taken by Hsi along the path of faith in God alone for this department of life. At first he stood almost alone. The other Christians could not understand his attitude. As they came more and more to apprehend spiritual principles, however, they were eventually willing to waive the advantages at their disposal through treaty rights and the protection to be obtained through the influence of foreigners, and commit their case to God only.

The same principle of meeting hostility and opposition with meekness and quietness proved its value in the progress of the refuge work. Sian, the capital of the neighboring province of Shensi, was at that time one of the most conservative and anti-foreign cities in China, and to open a refuge there, with the object of making known the gospel, required wisdom as well as courage. Hsi was convinced that it must be done, however, and premises were obtained and opened – and they remained open! D. E. Hoste, who followed all its progress with prayer and the keenest interest, wrote to Hudson Taylor about it.

> "Mr. Hsi read me two or three exceedingly interesting letters from Sian. You may recollect that some time ago they were helped in getting premises by a Mohammedan military M.A. who broke off his opium with them. Well, at the recent examination two young scholars who were trying for the degree met their old friend, this Mohammedan, and were at once surprised to see how well he looked. They found out that he had given up his opium pipe, and on asking how this was, were told of the refuge. Accordingly, at the close of the examination, they entered as patients, made rapid progress towards being freed from the habit, and in about two weeks left the refuge full of gratitude. At first, being wealthy men, sons of a retired official, they pressed twenty taels on the man in charge as a token of gratitude; but on this being absolutely refused, they insisted, in spite of all remonstrances, in putting up a tablet on the front

door, on which the account of their deliverance from the opium habit, together with a statement that this was due to the power of heaven, was briefly written out. In a city where the official classes have hitherto been so hostile the above is certainly very encouraging.

The policy which the brethren there have pursued by Mr. Hsi's direction has been to avoid exciting the prejudice and opposition of neighbors by public preaching and praying, whilst seeking by private prayer, gentleness, and honesty towards all men, to disarm suspicion, looking to God to give them acceptance with the people, and establish them in the place.

To what extent D. E. Hoste was responsible for the increasingly high spiritual tone of the church and its leader, it is impossible to say. That Pastor Hsi consulted with him in all matters relating to policy there is no doubt, for he completely won the confidence and love of his Chinese colleague. But it was not won quickly or easily. The years at Hungtung were years of discipline for the young missionary. Not only had he to exercise much patience with the Chinese leader, but to endure the quiet disapproval of some missionaries who could not understand his attitude and felt he should have taken a stronger line. But when, one day, Pastor Hsi came to him, burdened to tears about some church problem, and said, "Ah! Pastor Hoste! I couldn't get on without you!" he thought to himself "Well! It's been worth it!"

The friendship between the two men, strengthened and purified by many hours of prayer and travail over souls, had also a very warm and human side.

Once, during a time of famine, D. E. Hoste heard that his Chinese colleague was living under conditions of great privation. Distressed at the news, he felt an immediate impulse to go to his succor. He had not much money by him, but took what he could, and set off on the long walk to Hsi's home. It was evidently an occasion when he failed to wait on the Lord for his guidance, for it was only as he was on his way that the unwelcome conviction came to him that he should not give the money! Probably there were a few times in his life when he was more strongly inclined to disobey his inward guide; for, undemonstrative as he was by nature, he was a man who truly loved his friends, and it grieved him to be unable to give help in this time of need. That he did the right thing by refraining was evident from Hsi's own testimony, given some while later, when the famine was over, of the special blessing that period of privation had been to him, and how a gift from the missionary at that time would have been a hindrance in the work. But the impulse so hardly resisted proves the warmth of D. E. Hoste's affection for the Chinese who had become so intimate a friend.

Hsi, on his part, showed equal concern for the things that affected the Englishman's personal life. When he heard that his father, General Hoste, was seriously ill, he was not content only to pray. He must *do* something. With great pains, therefore, he prepared some pills, two large pint-and-a-half bottles of them, requesting that they be forwarded to England. With the pills was a beautifully written letter, giving instructions to the effect that *eight* of the red pills were to be taken every evening with boiling water, and *twenty* of the black variety each morning after breakfast!

While his most intimate friendship was with Pastor Hsi, however, there were others who meant much to D. E. Hoste. His regard did not show itself so much in a warm demonstration of affection as in a faithful and sustained interest in the activities and lives of those who were his friends. One simple old countryman named Li Pu-ch'eo, whom he came to know and to love while in Shansi province, still had a place in his heart years later when, as general director of the Mission, it would not have been surprising had he forgotten him. He was a good friend to those who won his confidence and esteem, whether missionary or Chinese – one who did not forget with the passing of the years. Some who were his fellow missionaries during his first term of service, and later retired from the mission field, still maintained a friendship with him which did not lapse because their paths separated. As young workers, they found him a sympathetic and congenial companion. Unusually prayerful and aware of spiritual movements as he was, he was well-balanced, giving due regard to the claims of mind and body as well as of soul. "I am myself more and more a believer in fresh air as a help in nearly everything!" he wrote once. He was careful to take exercise by having a good walk each day, and kept himself informed of current affairs by reading a weekly newspaper sent out from home.

One who was his junior missionary for a time writes of him:

> What a kind, loving heart he had! Possibly many at Shanghai who knew him only as director of the Mission did not see this side of his character.
>
> When at home on the mission station, Mr. Hoste and I had many long walks, usually in the afternoons. On those walks we had profitable and interesting conversations, for he was a great conversationalist. I often heard him speak of his mother, also his father and his brothers. When we had walked a few miles we would get to some quiet spot where we had prayer together over the work and any matter specially laid on our hearts.
>
> He spent much of his time going round villages and hamlets in South Shansi where there were small churches. Those attending services were mostly poor farmers. He was quite at home with those humble people, and ate such things as they could provide, and was greatly loved. I went round all the villages and churches in Hungtung and Yoyang district for nearly four years after he left Shansi, and to the last the Christians were always talking about him, praying for him, and hoping he would come back.

The work in Hungtung grew steadily. Those who visited the church there were impressed by the reverence in the services and the attention paid to the messages. While there was not again a spectacular "draught of fishes" as during the spring of 1887, when over 200 were baptized, simple reports in *China's Millions* give evidence of quiet progress:

May, 1889

Over 400 men and women have been cured on these premises alone during the past autumn and winter season. Of these, over twenty families have put away idols and are learning the truth, and over 100 individual men and women whose families objected to the putting away of the household gods, having given up the worship of them themselves, and attend our worship, besides praying in private.

February, 1891

The work at Hungtung progresses quietly but steadily, much care being exercised in the reception of candidates for baptism, of whom, as will be seen, there was a large number recently.

December, 1891

Two days ago we baptized nearly fifty people here and had a happy time of worship.

October, 1893

Considering the Hungtung district as a whole, there is great cause for thanksgiving. Altogether, 51 persons were baptized last year.

By the year 1896, when Hsi died and D. E. Hoste returned home on furlough, the membership at Hungtung was larger than that of any other church in the province.

But what of the personal life of the missionary during those years? Often alone, without a fellow countryman to encourage him and strengthen his hands during times of difficulty, was he never downcast? Those who are actively engaged in the deliverance of souls from the bondage of Satan will never go for long without being themselves attacked.

"What solemn work really being engaged in God's service is!" he wrote. "It does bring one into close contact with tremendous powers of darkness. 'Keep me as the apple of thine eye, hide me under the shadow of thy wings,' 'Lead me in a plain path because of mine enemies' are two petitions that have come to me with an increasing sense of their fitness, even in my small measure of service and conflict. All the kingdoms of devils are, after all, under the power of our Father, and only afford means through which the perfect counsel and will of God can be unfolded."

From the very commencement of his missionary life he had been brought into contact with unusually brilliant and gifted workers. He had seen the wonderful power manifested at meetings when other members of the Cambridge Seven spoke. He had seen the exceptional quickness with which Stanley Smith got a grip of the Chinese language. Now his companion in the work was the masterful and enterprising Pastor Hsi. D. E. Hoste must often have been conscious that his own reserved nature and lack of eloquence put him very much in the background in comparison with these more attractive personalities. No envy of their gifts seems to have disturbed him, and in his letters there is a note of sincere joy as he recounts the spiritual triumphs of others. It would be surprising, however, if no paralyzing sense of inferiority ever oppressed him. Indeed, we know it did. He found himself gripped by one of those dark fears which sometimes assail missionaries. He feared he had made a mistake in coming to China.

Only those who have themselves known a similar experience can understand something of the anguish of soul through which he passed at that time. The assurance of being in the will of God is sometimes the steadying factor which brings the believer through circumstances which would otherwise be too much for him. Let that assurance be withdrawn, and the sweetest joys that life can offer are utterly inadequate to give peace of mind.

As he thought back over the past, he was honestly convinced that there had been nothing wrong in his motives in coming to China. He had been sincere and deeply in earnest. "But I felt," he said, when speaking of that dark experience in after years, "that I was not good enough." And now, what was to be done? He seriously considered giving up missionary work and returning to England; but he remembered the widespread interest stirred up by the going forth of the Cambridge Seven. He thought of the great meetings in which he had taken part. How could he go back so soon afterwards, an acknowledged failure?

How long this struggle lasted is uncertain, but it ended at length when his attention was directed no longer on himself, his inadequacy and impotence, but upon the one who was sowing such seeds of doubt in his mind. "An enemy hath done this." At last he saw the matter in its true light. He had been called and commissioned by God to serve him in China – and the devil for whose kingdom he had come to contend was resisting him, not openly, but with the subtlety of the serpent. The realization of this fact liberated his mind from the distress into which it had been brought. And, as always happens in such cases, he was better equipped for his future service than he would have been had he not had the experience. In contacts with young missionaries in later years, he was able to forewarn them of this special form of attack to which they themselves would almost certainly be subjected sooner or later in their service.

1890 dawned. The year held a sorrow of a very personal and intimate nature for D. E. Hoste, about which his fellow missionaries knew nothing at the time. Gertrude Broomhall, eldest daughter of Hudson Taylor's favorite sister, Amelia, returned to England from China so broken in health that it was feared she could never return.

The story of his love for her went back to their first meeting, on one of his earliest visits to Pyrland Road. Already preparing to go to China, she was then helping her father, Benjamin Broomhall, with his work as secretary of the Mission. The young recruit, usually so slow to make a decision, knew as he saw her sitting at her desk, head bent over her writing, that if ever there was to be a Mrs. D. E. Hoste, this rather delicate looking, fair-haired girl was she.

Why he waited as long as he apparently did before asking her to marry him is somewhat of a mystery, for they were often working in the same province and must have met frequently. Perhaps it was his characteristic hesitancy to take any step before being convinced that it was the Lord's will that deterred him. Perhaps he thought he was not good enough! When eventually he did tell her of his desire, she was already in such poor health that return to England was essential; and, uncertain as to whether she would ever be strong enough to return, she refused to marry him. For both of them the claim of God upon their lives ranked higher than any other, and God had called him to China. She sailed for home, while he, with a heart that must sometimes have been very desolate, turned steadfastly to his work.

D. E. Hoste, bachelor in Shansi

Chapter Six

Marriage and Furlough

IT was in December of the same year that a fellow worker was sent to him. Few people are more impressionable than new missionaries, and this young American remembered vividly the sixteen months he spent in Hungtung as D. E. Hoste's junior worker. He had already spent six months in the language school in Anking when Hudson Taylor went there to designate the new recruits to their different spheres of service.

"On Dr. Taylor's last day at Anking," he wrote, "he was to take passage on a Yangtze River steamer. He invited me to accompany him down to the river bank, where we awaited the arrival of the steamer. This period of waiting gave us ample time for fellowship and consultation about many matters concerning my future in China. Finally, Dr. Taylor said to me, 'I have corresponded with Mr. Frost [American Director of the C.I.M.] about you, and I believe Hungtung in the province of Shansi is the place where you will be happy and where you are most needed. Mr. D. E. Hoste, one of the Cambridge Band, is living there alone. He ought to have a helper, and I believe you can be that helper.... Mr. Hoste's life in England, as the son of an officer of high rank in the British Army, did not give him much opportunity to develop household skill in adapting himself to conditions of Chinese life. I understand you Americans are very adaptable to any situation in which you are placed, and you can be very helpful to Mr. Hoste in seeing that he has some of the home comforts to which we have been accustomed. Do what you can to help him have a varied menu, in order that his health may not be impaired by conforming too strictly to the Chinese diet. He is a deeply spiritual man, a great Bible student, and he will help you to adapt yourself to Chinese life and methods. Only be sure that you do not follow his lead and "go Chinese" too far, particularly in the matter of food.'

"Apparently some of Mr. Hoste's missionary friends were fearful he was conforming too closely to Chinese customs, and that in time his health would suffer as a result. I infer that these reports were made known to Mr. Taylor. It might possibly have been for this reason that I was chosen to go to Hungtung."

It is interesting to learn what were the impressions that the new missionary, just out from home, received of this his first senior. It sometimes happens that there is a sense of disappointment when an enthusiastic young worker arrives at his mission station, only to find a lower standard of life and work than he had expected. The keen edge of a willingness for sacrifice is easily blunted by observing a tendency to sloth and self-indulgence on the part of older workers. Little wonder that the first designations of new missionaries are the subjects of special prayer! No such disappointment awaited D. E. Hoste's junior worker, however.

"Upon arrival in Hungtung I found that Mr. Hoste had placed himself in the hands of Chinese servants, and that his meals were largely selected, cooked, and managed by them. He was a man who accepted the principle, 'When in Rome do as the Romans do.' He lived like the Chinese, conforming to their social and living customs to a greater degree than most missionaries of his day. As he lived alone as a bachelor, his home had almost nothing of the customary English atmosphere, such as imported furniture, curtains, and furnishings might impart. This does not mean that he was an ascetic. I adopted his standard of living, and found it amply sufficient for health and comfort.

"I had been with him but a very short time before he suggested that I assume the responsibility for the marketing and the preparation and serving of all the meals. I have always wondered if this suggestion had not come from Mr. Taylor, but never questioned Mr. Hoste in regard to the subject. Since he was the senior missionary, it was my duty to take over such responsibilities in the station as he assigned to me. I endeavored to vary the rather restricted menus. Mr. Hoste seemed to be much pleased with the changes made, and, I think, enjoyed them.

"The rooms in which we lived were situated on opposite sides of a fairly large open court, some thirty feet wide and nearly twice as long. Each of these apartments consisted of a long living room, and partitioned off at one end was a small bedroom. The table on which we had our meals was, at the beginning, situated in Mr. Hoste's living room; but as soon as he placed the responsibility for the meals upon me, he suggested that we should dine in my apartment. The table on which we had our meals was then placed in my room. After our breakfast and our period of Bible study and communion, Mr. Hoste would retire to his apartment across the court for a long period of prayer. He would close the large front doors and usually would spend some hours in intercessory prayer and Bible study. He usually prayed aloud, but in a very low tone, and would pace up and down the room while he was in prayer. He talked freely about prayer, and I enquired why he walked to and fro during those periods of communion with the Father. His reply was that somehow he seemed to have more freedom in prayer while walking – that prayer seemed more free and unrestrained. During his many journeys through the country to outlying villages and cities, he frequently sent his boy ahead with the donkey and baggage for some distance, while he followed behind on foot and prayed as he walked."

The young missionary was impressed by his senior worker's attitude towards Pastor Hsi, and found himself heartily approving of it.

"Mr. Hoste often said that Pastor Hsi, who was a very spiritually-minded man, and who was honored by all the missionaries and Christians, should be recognized as the real spiritual leader, not alone in the work of establishing and managing refuges, but also in the churches, which naturally resulted as men were converted through their trust in God to assist them in breaking off the power of opium.

"Therefore Mr. Hoste felt that he should recognize Pastor Hsi as the spiritual leader of the churches, and cooperate with him as such, and I always believed that he was very wise in doing this. He was criticized by some because they thought he was taking a secondary place, or making himself subservient to Pastor Hsi. As a matter of fact, Mr. Hoste was about two generations ahead of other missionaries in the matter of placing responsibility for church leadership upon wise and devoted Chinese Christians where the proper qualities of leadership were apparent.

"At the same time, the missionaries who criticized him were good friends of his. He was always welcomed to their homes. I never knew of any misunderstanding between him and any of his fellow missionaries. He seemed to be very friendly with all, and would make occasional visits to them. I never heard of his having a friend that he did not retain.

"At the time I lived with him one of the Cambridge Band had severed his relationship with the Mission and was working in a station some two or three days' journey to the east of Hungtung. Mr. Hoste visited him, and stayed with him for several days, returning much refreshed over his renewal of their earlier close relationship. He much enjoyed social intercourse with fellow missionaries."

But what attracted the young missionary to his senior perhaps more than anything else was his quiet confidence in God.

"I do not recall his ever being morose or cast down. Sometimes he was very serious in his conversation, very much in earnest, but always trustful and triumphant."

But in spite of the companionship of a fellow worker and the evident improvement effected in his living conditions, the summer of 1891 found him with a sense of weariness which he could not altogether overlook.

T'angchen, 45 Miles N.W. of Hungtung

On recovering from an attack of illness, I paid a visit to Hochow. Then, some six weeks ago, I came up here, and have been having a very nice time in this quiet spot. Our premises here stand on a flat and table-like height overlooking the little market town, which at this distance looks picturesque, with its heavy roofs sloping at all angles, and here and there one of those queer, elaborately top-heavy little towers which abound in these parts. One finds the quiet loneliness of the pine-clad hills and the ripening crops of autumn grain very soothing and refreshing, more so than in days when one was more buoyant and vigorous.

The following year there was a famine in Shansi. What this meant to the missionaries is difficult adequately to describe. The continual sight of suffering, seeing people dying of starvation, and being unable to help more than a very few, cannot but be a strain on those who love their fellow men.

But God is full of compassion, and his tender mercies are over all his works. Although he may suffer his people to hunger, whether for judgment or discipline, he delights to satisfy them. The months passed, and the rain came. Once more the green blades of young corn forced their way up through the earth, this time to ripen to the expected harvest. And away in England health was returning to a weary body and tired nerves. In 1893 the door to China was opened once more, and before the year ended Gertrude Broomhall was back.

Some months after she returned, a conference for missionaries, arranged to coincide with Hudson Taylor's visit to the province, provided an opportunity for D. E. Hoste to meet her again. Here they became engaged, and then events moved swiftly. Hudson Taylor was planning to travel to Tientsin, and he suggested that they should join his party, accompanying him to that city, so that they could get married there. So it came about that in the October number of *China's Millions* a cryptic paragraph announced:

> By a wire received on 5th Sept. from Tientsin – presumably from Mr. Hudson Taylor – Mr. and Mrs. Broomhall heard of the intended marriage, on the following Thursday, of their daughter Gertrude, to Mr. D. E. Hoste. We feel sure that this news will be received with much interest by all those to whom our friends are personally known.

Very happily they entered upon their life together. Returning to Hungtung a few days before his bride, D. E. Hoste was able to get the home ready to receive her; and when she arrived she found the rooms gay with flowered curtains, and with a Chinese scroll from the church members on which were inscribed in gold characters the words, "With one heart serve the Lord."

"We are both well and very happy," wrote Gertrude Hoste. "The Lord himself is drawing us closer and closer into a very blessed heart union." This was not effected all at once, however, as she revealed many years afterwards. She did not always find her husband easy to understand. She noticed that when they prayed together he often asked that they might be helped to love one another, and not unnaturally this puzzled and rather hurt the new bride! Why did he pray thus? she asked him eventually. Did they not already love one another?

"Yes," he replied quietly. "We do. But Satan always attacks that which is of God."

The suitability of the union became increasingly apparent with the passing of the years. From her earliest days, Gertrude Broomhall had lived in the very heart of the Mission; and her intimate knowledge, both of its principles and of the peculiar problems in its administration, fitted her in an unusual way to be the wife of the man who became its director. Although physically not strong, and unable to do much active work, she possessed sympathy and gentleness of manner which drew confidences and smoothed out misunderstandings in a way her husband, more austere and reserved, would have found difficult, if not impossible. He often spoke of the help she was to him and the strength of her prayer-fellowship. In her the man who was destined to tread the lonely path of leadership always had one to whom he could tell the inmost secrets of his heart. It is doubtful if he ever did so to any other.

Very shortly after his wedding, D. E. Hoste received a letter from Hudson Taylor asking him to take over the superintendency of the work in the southwest of Shansi, in addition to continuing to fulfill his duties as missionary in charge of Hungtung. This meant that he would be expected to attend periodic meetings of the China Council in Shanghai; and so, at the age of thirty-four, the youngest member present, he took his seat for the first time in the assembly in which he was later to occupy the most prominent and responsible position for thirty-five years, and through which he was to direct and influence the life and work of the whole Mission.

"His contributions to the discussion of the subjects on the agenda," wrote one who was present on that occasion, "even thus early in his missionary career, gave evidence of his grasp of principles, and revealed that he possessed the faculty that discerns the germane."

But the additional strain of the new work, coming at the end of his first term of service, was too much for his tired brain and highly-strung system. He began to find it difficult to concentrate; and his mind, so well disciplined, no longer seemed able to respond to his will. Thoughts that he fain would banish persisted in harassing him. Perhaps only those who have experienced it can understand the real anguish of soul such a condition can cause one whose chief desire is an unsullied life with God. The concern it occasioned him can be sensed in a letter, mainly concerned with Shansi mission news, in which he confided his problem to Hudson Taylor.

Hungtung, Shansi
4th Feb., 1896

My Dear Uncle,

It is with much pleasure that I find myself able to settle down to write to you. First let me thank you, on behalf of Gertie as well as myself, most heartily for your very kind and generous Christmas gift. It touched me so much that you and dear Aunt should thus remember us in the midst of your thronging duties and difficulties. Your love and friendship are to me most precious, and your words and actions constantly come up to me in times of perplexity, with help and guidance; and this fact has again been an encouragement to me, when oppressed with a sense of how little I seem able to do in guiding and influencing others, for just as many, many words and acts of yours, noticed by me at different times have since been used by the Spirit to me, so if only I am with God, my influence may, in its measure, tell. I do long to be godlier. It seems so sad that the heart should wander from God and want other things. As this is a private and personal letter I want to ask your prayer and advice as to what is to me a great source of distress and perplexity in my inner life. I find that in prayer wandering thoughts come in; and then in confessing them, often more wandering thoughts come; and in this way often quite a considerable time will be taken up in a desperate struggle to get clear of the various thoughts, and fix the heart and mind in an unwavering concentration on God. You can understand how exhausting this is for one's head; and really now by the time one has been able to pray believingly for them all, one's head is often throbbing, and one is quite wearied. When I see how many are, owing to neglect of private prayer, gross and heavy and more or less blind, I dare not give it up.

Mails were slow in those days, and weeks passed before he received a reply. Hudson Taylor, pressed as he was with work, had little time to spare for writing long letters. In one sentence he told, with simple sincerity, how he himself had learned to pray without strain:

"Regarding a wandering mind in prayer: I have found more help in praying aloud, and praying while walking about – talking as to a present Lord – than in any other way."

Nevertheless, that was not all the missionary veteran wrote. He himself had borne burdens too great for his own natural strength, and knew well what it was to be "pressed beyond measure." What comfort the younger man, oppressed with a sense of spiritual weakening, must have gained from the next sentence:

"I do not think that wandering in thought at all necessarily indicates a loss of spiritual life, but it does show a loss of nerve tone and calls for ... use of such measures as will generally give vigor to the health."

That was all the reference Hudson Taylor made to D. E. Hoste's problem then, but he evidently did not forget it. The man who was indeed the father of the Mission had suffered himself from the attacks of Satan upon a mind that had become faint and wearied. His own experiences along that line made him quick to recognize when another was in need. He understood, as did his Divine Master before him, how to treat tired workers. "Come ye yourselves apart, and rest awhile." And so it came about that in May of that year D. E. Hoste set out for England on his first furlough.

Those who are to be of real spiritual help to others must be prepared for peculiar trials and tests, that the qualities of endurance and adherence to principle, sympathy and understanding may be wrought out in them.

> I learnt
> The fullest measure of obedience – learnt
> The wide, deep love, embracing all mankind,
> Passing through all the phases of their woe,
> That I before their God might plead for all.

There is no easy shortcut to spiritual maturity. The path to perfection is by suffering. Furlough meant most welcome relief from the problems and responsibilities of his post on the mission field, but it also involved a trial of another sort, for his wife and their baby son must be left behind in China. Just when he was perhaps most conscious of needing the one who completely understood and loved him, he must go alone.

There was nothing arbitrary or unfeeling about this decision on the part of Hudson Taylor. He felt the frequent separations from his own wife and family too keenly not to sympathize with others who had to make a similar sacrifice. But Gertrude Hoste had only returned from furlough about three years, and those who join the China Inland Mission do so prepared to set aside personal interests and claims when these cut across the progress of the gospel. It is understood that both husbands and wives are missionaries, and that there may be times when separations of shorter or longer duration will be necessary, in order that the work be not hindered. There were others on the field at the time who were needing furlough, but who, because there was no one to take their place, were unable to leave. Had she accompanied her husband, it might have given rise to dissatisfaction, as well as causing criticism at home. They must walk so as to give no offense, either to unbeliever, brother, or the church of God.

Hoste sailed as far as Colombo with Hudson Taylor and his wife, leaving them there to spend a few weeks with a brother living in India. It is interesting to know what sort of impression he made on one who had not seen him for ten years. It was his humility more than anything else that his brother observed – humility in little things. In India, where race and caste count for so much, it was an unusual thing to see a white man, with instinctive courtesy, step aside to allow a poor coolie a clear path!

While in India, a serious attack of fever further lowered his vitality, and on his arrival in England it became increasingly apparent that the prolonged strain of life in inland China had taken a heavy toll of his health. Greatly needing rest from all the mental strain attendant on those who have constantly to speak at meetings and make contact with a number of people, he went to Scotland, hoping that the opportunity for quiet, combined with healthy exercise in the fresh air, would ease his weariness and renew his strength. This time typhoid fever laid him low, and by the time he had recovered from that his condition was little better than it had been when first he reached home. He was quite unfit to return to China. It was therefore arranged that he should visit Australia, on the one hand for the sake of his health, and on the other that his wife might join him and help in deputation work in that country. In May, therefore, a letter was sent from Hudson Taylor to a friend in Adelaide, making arrangements for his reception there.

> My nephew, Mr. Hoste, is about to visit Australia, sailing in June by P. and O. I think it would be well for him to break his

Marriage and Furlough

journey in Adelaide and spend a month or two there. I believe your healthy climate would do very much to restore his vigor. As you will probably know, he was one of the Cambridge Seven. His father, General Hoste, has another son for twelve years on the Congo, while another was for several years engaged in missionary work in Paris. Mr. Hoste has not merely been pulled down by work in China, but had a serious attack of fever in Ceylon on his way home, and typhoid fever in Scotland last autumn. Though not able to do very much perhaps at first in the way of meetings, I think his presence in the colony would be a help to your missionary interests, and especially that of his wife, who will join him from China. She is an admirable speaker.

Could you make arrangements for his reception on arrival, and assist him in making inexpensive arrangements for boarding? I wonder if Mr. Finlayson would allow them to board and pay for their board with him for a time; the quiet of their country home would be very helpful to a wearied brain. I mention him because when I was in Adelaide he urged me to send any weary missionary to him; but six or seven years may have brought in great changes, and this might be now quite unsuitable. Mrs. Hoste's little boy will be about two years old. Could you give me any idea what economical board would be likely to cost them in Adelaide – which I imagine is much healthier than the neighborhood of Melbourne? I hope I am not taxing you too much; it will be a great comfort to Mr. Hoste to be met on arrival, or to be able easily to find someone who has been in China.

Yours affectionately,
J. HUDSON TAYLOR

It was only about seven years since a China Inland Mission council had been formed in Australia. The strengthening of the ties between the workers on the field and the home councils in North America, Australia and Europe was a matter of paramount importance to Hudson Taylor, knowing how much the progress of the gospel in China depended upon the prayers and cooperation of those at the home bases. Even he, however, could have had no idea of the value of this particular visit, for at that time it is doubtful whether he had any thought of making D. E. Hoste his successor. So often it is only in retrospect that the overruling hand of God is clearly seen. At the time it must have seemed that the missionary was needed far more in China than in Australia, and only in after years did it appear how much was gained by the General Director having had the intimate contact with Mission leaders in Australasia which his prolonged stay there afforded.

Shortly after his arrival there in July, 1897, he wrote to Mrs. Hudson Taylor:

> I found myself very weak and below par on landing, but have been getting better latterly, by dint of keeping quite quiet. Everyone is very kind, and I hope on Gertie's arrival to go up to Belair and stay at Hope Lodge with Mr. and Mrs. Morton. Their house is in a beautiful situation on the hills, and I look forward much to being there with my dear wife and son. How thankful I am that our separation is at length coming to an end!

Progress in health was made very slowly. In November, writing to Hudson Taylor, he reported:

"I have found that my head is still easily made bad again; though when I live quietly and without much brain-work, the symptoms of congestion are scarcely ever felt; and this is a great advance upon my condition in England."

In spite of weariness, however, he was not idle, and the little family was rarely in one place for long:

> We have been taking several meetings lately, and have just returned from five or six days in Adelaide.... I hope soon to visit two or three places up the country, where Mr. Powell, our local secretary, is arranging for a few meetings.... Our purpose is to leave here towards the end of November, and after a short time in Melbourne to go on to Tasmania.

This prolonged stay in Australasia was probably one of the happiest periods of his life. He was free from responsibility, such as he had had in Shansi, and which he was to know in increasing measure in the thirty-seven years of missionary service which, unknown to himself, lay before him. Many quiet hours were spent in the shady public gardens in Melbourne, where he and his wife sat watching their child at play. And as they sat there, thankful for the gradual return of health and vigor, they prayed.

"This stay in Australia," he wrote to Hudson Taylor, "has been just one long lesson that 'he gives the very best to those who leave the choice with him.' Right through we have seen our Father's care for us in providing us with kind friends and surroundings suitable for our need. It has been strengthening indeed to our faith, and we do pray that after all this time of special love and kindness of the Lord in giving us bodily rest and comfort, we may not fail to walk in his path if it means trial, discomfort, and privation sometimes, in order that the gospel may be brought to the Chinese."

Meanwhile, the time was drawing near for return to China. It had been assumed that the Hostes would return to their old province of Shansi. It was evident, however, that there was greater need of them elsewhere, and they were asked to go to Honan in order to superintend the work there.

It is interesting to observe D. E. Hoste's reaction to the suggestion that he should not, after all, return to Shansi. In a letter to Hudson Taylor he wrote:

> Whilst, of course, on some grounds it would be a very real trial to us both not to go back there, there are some considerations that would make the prospect of work in another part of China very welcome. Enlarged experience and widened knowledge of God's work are things to be thankful to get, though at the cost of losing some of the closeness of old ties.

His was a mind that ever reached out to acquire more knowledge. It was always the intellectual rather than the aesthetic that appealed to him, and he was not an emotional man. A keen observer, he seemed to retain all he saw and read, applying it to the practical issues of life. To him, therefore, there was a zest in going where he would have opportunity to exercise further the active mind that he had consecrated so wholly to the service of God.

Yet it was with a deep sense of his own insufficiency that he went to the new sphere of service. "I feel much cast upon God," he wrote to Mrs. Hudson Taylor, "and value the prayers of Uncle and yourself much." Few men ever distrusted themselves more than he.

In Honan he introduced no radical changes or reforms in the work and thereby avoided arousing the sense of resentment that enthusiastic and enterprising men so often create when they take over leadership. His influence was felt more by what he was than by what he did.

"He made a great impression upon me and all of the missionaries by his prayer life and wise counsel," wrote F. S. Joyce, who later became superintendent of the province. "He looked at matters concerning the work and the Chinese workers from the Chinese point of view. He emphasized the principles and practices of the Mission regarding simplicity of life, enduring hardship for Christ's sake, and honoring the Chinese. And he gave us a fine example in the way he observed them himself.

"He always carried a burden for perishing souls in his heart. Evangelism was *everything* to him."

His clarity of thought and quiet grasp of principle, however, were bringing him more and more into prominence at the quarterly council meetings in Shanghai. His quiet, unimpassioned contributions to the discussions there were such that Hudson Taylor once said they ought to be written in letters of gold. The time was drawing near when he was to be thrust into the position he was to occupy for thirty-five years.

Chapter Seven

Leader of the Mission

THE Boxer Rising of 1900 will never be forgotten in the history of the China Inland Mission. The antipathy of the Chinese to the foreign powers had been provoked by the encroachments – mainly of Germany, Russia, and France – on the territory of their land. The revolutionary ideas of certain reformers further assailed the conservative spirit of old China, and when the dowager empress seized the reins of government from the youthful emperor, who was being swayed by the reformers' suggestions, it needed but a match to set alight a conflagration so widespread as to affect missionaries and Chinese Christians in the remotest regions of the great land.

The Patriotic Volunteers, known as the Boxers, provided the match. These men, cruel and fanatical, banded themselves together for the destruction of all foreigners in the country and those who were associated with them in the propagation of the "foreign religion," as Christianity was called. Backed by the dowager empress herself, the decree went forth that they were to be destroyed. From all parts of the country missionaries and their children sought to escape, many of them enduring incredible hardships as they traveled hundreds of miles to the coast. That so many came through alive was little short of miraculous. But for some was reserved the high honor of sealing their testimony with their blood, and before the terrible rising was eventually suppressed, fifty-eight members of the Mission and twenty-one children had been brutally murdered.

What must have been the horror and anguish of heart of those living at the Mission headquarters in Shanghai as they received report after report of fellow workers being heartlessly assaulted and massacred it is impossible to imagine. For over thirty years the Mission had faced all the danger of life in a country with age-old prejudices against foreigners. Mission premises had been attacked, and missionaries themselves had not always come through unscathed. Yet with the one exception of a worker who was murdered amongst the tribespeople of southwest China, members of the Mission had been wonderfully protected amidst many dangers from the beginning. And now the forces of evil seemed let loose, and blow after blow fell as news came through of those in the interior who had been trapped and done to death.

To make matters worse, Hudson Taylor, whose presence and leadership at such a time would have been a strength to all, was away in Switzerland, suffering from severe overstrain. The brunt of the burden fell on J. W. Stevenson, his deputy, and glad he was to have D. E. Hoste at his side. Hudson Taylor, little knowing how great the need would be for his support, had suggested that he remain in Shanghai with his wife and children during the summer, in order to render what help he could, and he was there when the storm broke.

It was in his loved province of Shansi that the fury of the Boxers reached its height, and by far the greatest number of those who were martyred died there. A glimpse of what this meant to him is given in a letter written at that time. In the midst of distress there was a surge of triumphant joy at the knowledge that so many of the Chinese amongst whom he himself had worked had proved faithful unto death to the Lord they loved.

> A telegram last night tells of the home-going to Christ of eleven more dear ones from Hsichu, Taning and Yoyang. I feel Shansi is honored, and my heart beats for her more than ever; and the tears come, too, as I think of so many – friends of early manhood – gone in blood and tears. What a great gathering from South Shansi "in that day"!

In the midst of the troubles, however, a message of quite another order came to him like a bolt from the blue, throwing him into a state of inward turmoil which lasted for weeks, if not months. The Boxer crisis made it evident to Hudson Taylor that there was need for someone to be vested with authority to decide matters in China without the delay which was inevitable when problems had to be referred to him. He realized, too, that even should his health improve temporarily, the time was drawing near when he could no longer maintain the leadership of the Mission. Were the matter of appointing his successor left in abeyance, the whole Mission would be thrown into a state of confusion when its founder and leader died.

On August 7th, therefore, a cable was received at headquarters in Shanghai from Hudson Taylor, appointing D. E. Hoste to the position of acting general director!

There seems little doubt from the reactions of both J. W. Stevenson and D. E. Hoste that this appointment was totally unexpected. That a successor to Hudson Taylor must sooner or later be found was, of course, evident; and indeed the thoughts of many had turned to one who seemed eminently suitable for the position. William Cooper had already been appointed to the position of visiting China director, this placing him on an equal footing with J. W. Stevenson, who had been Hudson Taylor's deputy for many years; it had seemed that the next step for him would be to the general directorship. But God had reserved for him some better thing. While traveling in the north, he was caught in the maelstrom of Boxer fury, and was amongst those whose high privilege it was to lay down their lives for Christ's sake.

And so the one who was surely God's choice for the leadership of the Mission received the cable which caused him and J. W. Stevenson both surprise and consternation. With unusual rapidity, D. E. Hoste made up his mind; and the following day a reply cable was sent to Hudson Taylor refusing the appointment!

In a letter he gave his reasons for doing so. By whatever name he was called, he said, he could really do no more than he was already doing, by prayer and advice, helping J. W. Stevenson.

> There are effects of ... a very grave character which both Mr. Stevenson and myself agree in thinking most likely, if not certain, to follow such an appointment. I cannot conceal from myself that in the eyes of many it would have the effect of weakening and to a certain extent discrediting Mr. Stevenson in his present position, without inspiring confidence or gaining acquiescence in myself or mine. In my humble opinion, Mr. Stevenson has been much helped and strengthened in his direction of affairs during this crisis, and such, I believe, is the feeling of the other members of the council here as well. On the other hand, I believe that my appointment to act now on your behalf would come as a complete surprise to them, and is one to which they would not agree. To sum up, I earnestly believe that my appointment to act on your behalf here during your present incapacity would be calculated to weaken and even produce disruption in the Mission. Therefore, I do most humbly and decidedly decline to accept it. Believe me that I write this with a solemn sense of my responsibility to the Lord, and to yourself, in so doing.

He had such a deep love and reverence for Hudson Taylor that it grieved him to have to go against his wish in such an important matter, and in the weeks following he was often disturbed in mind. On September 24th he wrote:

> I need not say much now as to how truly I feel unworthy of and unequal to such a position; I do not feel it enough, I expect; but still, I do have a very deep sense of how I am indeed unfit. You will have received my letter in reply to your telegram; and whilst at times I have felt troubled lest I should have grieved and disappointed you ... I can assure you I wrote with the truest desire to be any help possible to you, and with the fullest loyalty to you. And I must say that time has served to confirm my view that I can best now assist the work as one of Mr. Stevenson's helpers and advisers; and that any other relation would, as things are, be a false one.

The thought uppermost in his mind seems to have been the effect his appointment as general director would have on

J. W. Stevenson. Hudson Taylor's deputy was older than he, his missionary experience wider, and for years he had been in an administrative position at Shanghai. It was one thing for him to serve under Hudson Taylor, the venerated and loved founder of the Mission; it was another to acknowledge a young man not yet forty years of age, only two years back from his first furlough, as acting general director! D. E. Hoste remembered too well his own experience in the early days in Shansi not to understand something of the struggle that must be going on in Stevenson's heart. If it had been hard then for him to take the position of junior under one who was his own contemporary, how much more difficult for an older and more experienced man to serve under *him!*

While this was, perhaps, the uppermost consideration in his mind, his refusal was based on something deeper than a fear of unfavorable reactions on the part of others. What oppressed him was a consciousness of his own unfitness for the position. "Beyond a deep attachment – wrought, I believe by the Lord – to dear Uncle himself, and also to the principles of our Mission," he wrote to Mrs. Hudson Taylor, "I must say I feel devoid of qualifications necessary for directing its affairs."

But God has His own ways of convincing his servants of his will and purpose for their lives. Those who are willing to obey him are rarely left long in doubt as to the path they should travel. In October D. E. Hoste was again laid low with an attack of typhoid fever, and with paralysis of arms and legs, caused by clots in the veins. Outward activities curtailed, he had the more time to think and pray; and as he did so the conviction grew in his heart that he should accept the appointment. Slowly and with evident reluctance, he made his decision. On November 15th he wrote to Hudson Taylor:

> Latterly I have been able to devote prayer and thought to the subject, and I now feel that I should, when restored to health, take steps to carry into effect your wish....

I cannot rid myself of the feeling that the position will be a very difficult and to some extent a false one for me and Mr. Stevenson; and in view of my illness I am led to hope that the Lord may yet raise you up more speedily than anticipated, and render the necessity of my appointment void. I know you will not mind my telling you freely how the thing seems to me. I trust during the coming fortnight to be much in prayer, and am sure I shall be guided and strengthened to carry out God's will. You know that I could conceive of no higher honor and privilege than being your helper, much more your representative or successor; and if God so lead, as in view of your letters I believe he will, I can only say it is but a fresh instance of how his ways are not our ways, and that his grace can triumph over the otherwise impossible, and that his strength really is made perfect in weakness.

A week later, in a letter to Mrs. Hudson Taylor in which he expressed his consciousness of being unworthy of the confidence her husband placed in him and unfit for the leadership of the Mission, he wrote:

However, I have confidence in the Lord that he will not suffer me to be placed in circumstances that will prove too much for the grace and strength that he will give. I have thought sometimes in years past that I was about as hard pressed as I well could be, and yet he in his mercy and tender grace pitied me, and did not suffer me to be crushed. Will you pray above all that I may be humble, and may really be kept from seeking my own glory and profit? And oh! for a baptism of the positive love of Christ for his people! Alas! how I need, how I long for a filling of the Spirit of Christ; merely not to seek my own will not be enough, I need the strong love of Christ to constrain me to spend and be spent for others. Will dear Uncle and you plead with God to baptize me with His Spirit?

Having at last been persuaded that he ought to accept the appointment from which he naturally shrank, he approached Stevenson. Without the deputy director's wholehearted acceptance of the situation, it would be impossible for the two of them to work together in the unity of heart and mind so essential for real spiritual success. But here he found that the Lord who humbled himself was able to impart the same grace to his disciple. None, probably, could sympathize with J. W. Stevenson's position more truly than D. E. Hoste; and it must have stirred him deeply when the older man, who for so long had been second only to Hudson Taylor in the Mission, told him with tears in his eyes that the Lord had given not only peace, but joy, in the assurance that the appointment was of God and would be for blessing.

"I have been not a little impressed with the eminently Christian spirit and largeness of mind which he has displayed in the course of our conversations together," Hoste wrote to Hudson Taylor. "I earnestly trust that this step, involving as it may seem to some an apparent diminution of his influence, may through your prayers and those of others, and the supply of the Spirit of Jesus Christ in him and me, prove to be greatly for its strengthening and extension.

"This, I know from your letter to me, is what you desire me to aim at; and I have further noted carefully, and shall endeavor to act upon your word as to my appointment not being intended to supersede Mr. Stevenson in his present position. I shall greatly value any instructions, whether as to details or indicating general lines of conduct for my guidance, more especially in my relation to him, and shall endeavor by God's help loyally to act upon them."

In January, 1901, therefore, Hudson Taylor formally appointed D. E. Hoste as acting general director of the Mission. The decision was received very favorably. From council members in China and the home countries came letters of approval. "The choice seems to me, so far as I can judge, an eminently suitable one." "The appointment of Mr. Hoste has been very warmly received." "I certainly know of no one in the Mission as well or better qualified for the directorship." "How very thankful we felt that Mr. Hoste consented to accept the position." "The council expressed its satisfaction at the appointment, believing that Mr.

Hoste has in a marked degree the gifts requisite for such a position." The testimony which perhaps expressed most adequately the feelings of those who knew him best was couched in the simple words "We needed a man who could give time to prayer, and thus get to know the mind of the Lord. I am most thankful that you have been led to select, it may be, the most prayerful man among us."

It was because of his prayerfulness, more than any other quality, that he gained and maintained the confidence of the members of the Mission throughout his thirty-five years' directorship. Bishop Frank Houghton, now general director himself, has written, "While Mr. Hoste, being human, was not immune from errors of judgment, yet criticism was silenced, dissatisfaction found no room to grow or spread, because our general director was a man who spent much time with God."

Nevertheless, it would be incorrect to say that there was no dissentient voice. One senior member of the Mission demurred at the appointment and raised the question of the general director being vested with final authority in Mission affairs. On this point Hudson Taylor was adamant. Before the Mission was formed he had given months of prayerful consideration to the matter of its government and administration, and felt so convinced that God had given him the pattern then that he could not go back on it. Indeed, over eighty years of Mission history, in which no fundamental change has taken place, have provided ample evidence that the plan was truly of God. In replying to the one who was dissatisfied, therefore, Hudson Taylor wrote with a firmness so tempered with gentleness and consideration that the very spirit of the man seems breathed into it:

> You, dear brother, joined the work many years ago, accepting the principle of directorship rule; and your continuing a member of the Mission is a testimony wherever it is known that you still at least can acquiesce in it. No one can remain in the membership of the Mission without recognizing Mr. Hoste as acting general director. I know him too well to fear

his attempting in any way to come between you and our Lord as supreme. I trust most sincerely that you will feel able to give him this recognition; but if not, I see no alternative to your retirement. We have been warm friends for long years, and my feeling towards you will remain the same whichever course you feel you should take. Should you feel unable to remain with us, you must still allow us to minister to your support, say for twelve months, to allow you time to find a position more in accordance with your present views.

How greatly Hudson Taylor was loved can be seen from a letter written by Henry Frost, who was then home director in America, to Mrs. Taylor. Expressing his approval of the appointment of D. E. Hoste, and affirming his loyalty to him, he went on to say:

> I must add that I say all this with deep sadness. My love is fixed preeminently upon Mr. Taylor, and it is hard to have any person come in between him and myself. The past thirteen years of fellowship, in which I have received from your husband nothing but tender and generous love, cannot be forgotten; and it is not easy to have the sweet exchange of this in any sense broken. But I bow before the will of God. Please do let me urge once more, however, that Mr. Taylor may not give up his office, and that no person be asked, so long as he lives, to be more than an assistant to him. This will make the coming change more bearable to me and to many others.

To take the position occupied by a man so loved and revered as Hudson Taylor would have been difficult for anyone. As founder of the Mission as well as its leader, his position in it was like that of a father to his family. No one could ever be to it what he had been. "Your relation to the work is unique," wrote D. E. Hoste, "and your feelings in regard to it likewise – more nearly what those of the Lord must be, than those of the rest of us." Few men, probably, have so perfectly manifested the fatherhood of God as Hudson Taylor, and few men have been so truly loved as he. D. E.

Hoste himself loved him with a devotion almost amounting to hero worship. What it must have meant to him to follow such a man it is only possible to surmise. The feeling of insufficiency and inferiority must have been almost overwhelming at times, and only the conviction that God had appointed him to the position would give him the quiet confidence that he needed.

As he entered upon his new responsibilities, he was faced with two major problems, the solutions to which would vitally affect the life of the Mission and its future effectiveness. Exactly how important a bearing they were to have upon the work perhaps even he did not fully comprehend at the time. "A little man to sort of steer," was his summing up of his own contribution to the work in Hungtung when he went there as a young missionary. Now he found himself filling the same need in the whole Mission. The direction he gave to the work, and the principles by which it was to be governed at this juncture, would determine the course taken in the years to come – and if there was a hair's breadth of deviation in the direction taken now, how far wide of the mark might not the future years find it!

The political crisis brought about by the Boxer Rising was already past. The besieged foreign legations in Peking had been relieved, the Imperial Court had fled, and the wise statesman, Li Hung-chang, was at the helm of his country's affairs, piloting her through the complications with foreign powers. Compensation for losses incurred by missionaries and Chinese Christians was offered, and it was on this matter that much thought and prayer were spent at Mission headquarters. What was the right attitude to adopt?

Hudson Taylor, writing from Switzerland, advised that no claim should be made for anything, but that where compensation for destroyed Mission property was offered, it should be accepted. "I feel," he wrote, "we hold these on trust for God's work." D. E. Hoste's judicial mind, however, viewed the subject from every angle; and as he did so he realized that here was an opportunity to manifest the spirit of Jesus Christ by a free forgiveness of those who had wronged them. On the other hand, "whilst our Lord teaches forgiveness to enemies, the action of the temporal government in vindication of law and order is also recognized as being of God," he wrote to Mr. Stevenson from Shansi, where he had gone with a commission to look into the matter with the governor of the province. Then again, the position of the Mission was different from that of the Chinese Christians, who as Chinese citizens were entitled to the protection and compensation afforded by the law of their country. He realized that the attitude taken now would have an important bearing on the work later on, and it was only after much prayerful discussion with his colleagues that he finally decided on his course of action.

The Chinese officials had invited the help of the commission in the matter of compensation, and a list of trustworthy men was drawn up to attend to the making out of claims. Those of the Chinese Christians were dealt with first. The representative of the Chinese Foreign Office wanted to deduct 20 or 30 percent from whatever was thus claimed, but D. E. Hoste demurred. To allow the deduction would be tantamount to admitting that the Christians were asking for more than their due, and he was adamant on that point. Law was in operation, and justice demanded payment to the uttermost farthing! Although the officials looked rather distressed, they had no option but to give full compensation to those who required it. They were told, however, that some remission would be made on the claims of the Mission.

At the next visit he paid them, D. E. Hoste presented a carefully made out estimate of the losses sustained by the Mission. But this time *grace* was in operation. Having presented the estimate, he announced that no payment would be accepted, for nothing was required! Forgiveness was full and free – the debt was wiped out! The full result of this practical manifestation of the spirit of Jesus Christ cannot well be assessed. The governor issued proclamations which were posted in all the churches in the province, announcing that no compensation was demanded or received for the losses incurred by the missionaries.

> The Mission, in rebuilding these churches with its own funds, aims in so doing to fulfill the command of the Savior of the world that all men should love their neighbors as themselves.... Contrasting the way in which we have been treated by the missionaries with our treatment of them, how can anyone who has the least regard for right and reason not feel ashamed of this behavior.... Jesus in His instructions inculcates forbearance and forgiveness, and all desire for revenge is discouraged.... From this time forward I charge you all, gentry, scholars, army and people, those of you who are fathers to exhort your sons, and those who are elder sons to exhort your younger brothers, to bear in mind the example of Pastor Hoste, who is able to forbear and to forgive, as taught by Jesus to do.

Property had been destroyed ruthlessly, yet no compensation was sought. Lives had been brutally taken, yet those whose loved ones had thus suffered came back willingly to continue telling the good tidings of a Savior's love. Such positive proof of the sincerity of the motives the missionaries had in coming to China could not be gainsaid. That one action was probably more effective in breaking down prejudice than years of zealous preaching would have been.

The other major problem threatening to affect the life of the Mission itself was not so easily solved. The Principles and Practices which had been so carefully drawn up years before are based upon what may be termed conservative evangelical truth. Those who join the Mission, whatever their denomination, must satisfy the council that they adhere to these fundamental doctrines. Faith in the living God who answers prayer, in the divine Savior whose sacrifice alone is the atonement for sin, in the Holy Spirit who imparts the new life, belief in the resurrection to eternal life of those who repent and 'believe, and the eternal loss of those who reject Christ – this faith is what is required of all who enter the Mission.

At the time of D. E. Hoste's appointment, one member of the Mission had embraced and was freely advocating a doctrine of the final restitution of all things, which the Mission could not accept. The question thus arose: what was to be the attitude of the directorate in such a case? Hoste saw clearly the importance of having the matter finally settled while Hudson Taylor, the founder of the Mission, was still alive; but as the discussion developed, it became clear that not only was there difference of opinion, but that the questions raised involved all the Mission councils – in Britain, America, Australasia, as well as in China. How to arrive at a solution which would satisfy all was a problem causing grave concern; and after much correspondence the director of the American council and the assistant director of the council for Great Britain were invited to Shanghai for conference.

It was a time of great stress for Hoste. In the weeks before the conference he had many apprehensions, for he was confronted with the possibility of disruption in the Mission right at the commencement of his office. So much did the long-drawn-out correspondence weigh upon his mind that he began to lose his sleep. Waking at two or three in the morning, he stayed awake, unable to rest. Writing to Hudson Taylor, he confessed:

> I feel deeply perplexed as to the right course to pursue in reference to attempting a settlement of the matter, and own to having felt serious misgivings ... lest I had made a mistake. I do not know whether I was right or not, but I simply cried to the Lord to pity his little child, and to undertake the matter, mistakes and all, and see us through. How sweet and blessed it is to take the Lord on this ground; I find it more and more. "The God of Jacob is our refuge." I like to say, "Yes, Lord, I admit all my blunders and folly and sins, but that is just the reason why I count upon thee to undertake the matter." "The Lord is very pitiful, and easy to be entreated, and does not upbraid."

What it all meant to him cannot well be assessed, for the one whose change of views had given rise to the whole discussion was a personal friend. The estrangement between them hurt him deeply, while the discussions and correspondence weighed much on his mind.

"I am feeling a good deal tired at times," he wrote. "I often wonder how I manage to keep on. It is a life of daily faith and drawing strength, physical and mental, as well as spiritual."

Nevertheless, although the storms of anxiety and apprehension disturbed him outwardly, he was conscious of an inward peace which was unassailable.

"I am feeling great rest of soul about the important council meetings in February," he wrote to Mrs. Hudson Taylor. "The Lord has drawn very near to me several times, and I believe that he is going to bind us all together as never before in our new relationships. A word that has been a help to me is, 'I will make all my mountains a way.'"

To Hudson Taylor he wrote:

> I cannot but think that the trials connected with this case have been a means of blessing to those concerned, in teaching the exercise of patience and forbearance; and I believe that they will turn out to be greatly to the strengthening and knitting together of those of us more intimately concerned in the administration of the Mission. I was much helped by the word in Joshua that it was not till the feet of the priests actually touched the water that the river divided. I believe the Lord gave me this as a promise, in connection with these discussions.

At last the council meetings commenced. Superintendents from various provinces in China and directors from America and Great Britain sat around the long table, with the new general director in the chair. There was almost an air of tension as these men who were conscious that they had been called together by the Lord himself for his service found themselves baffled over a point on which they could not agree. Without heart unity they could not work together. Was their fellowship to be broken up? Sometimes it seemed almost inevitable. But One who is perfect in knowledge was with them. As the discussion continued through many hours, the solution to the problem which had involved them in so much heart-searching and distress of mind was found. How simple it was, after all! The Mission that had always acknowledged directorship rule would continue to do so, but the directors should govern in accordance with basic principles, not arbitrarily.

The tension in the council room was snapped, and with an almost overwhelming sense of relief those present knelt down together to praise the Lord. How the prayers flowed out from thankful hearts! Then they rose to their feet and exultingly sang the Doxology! And in the minutes was recorded in a simple sentence the resolution:

"It was agreed that we record our continued conviction that the doctrinal basis of the Mission, as hitherto existing, should be maintained; and it is understood that, whilst the discretionary action of the directors in dealing with individual cases affecting doctrine amongst members of the Mission is to be exercised, such action shall be in view of and in harmony with the said doctrinal basis."

At the same time the decision was reached that any member of the Mission departing from the doctrinal basis would be required to resign.

Top: D. E. Hoste in his early forties, about the time of his appointment as general director by Hudson Taylor. Above: Mrs. D. E. Hoste

Chapter Eight

Building on the Foundations

From the time he became general director, D. E. Hoste's life became almost entirely absorbed in that of the Mission. Its history was his history. No records remain of the inner conflicts, the joys and sorrows of his heart during the years of his leadership. With almost startling suddenness a curtain seems to have been drawn across the sanctuary of his personal life. If he kept a private diary, it has never come to light. To Hudson Taylor, the man whom he loved and revered more than any other, he wrote freely; but in 1905 that true servant of God passed on to his reward, and D. E. Hoste was left with no one to whom he could turn for advice and guidance – no one but God.

What he meant to the Mission, and through it to the church of God in China, cannot be estimated. Although he was general director, his was to a great extent a hidden ministry. He did not become a public man in the same sense as his predecessor. His clarity of thought and expression was seen to better advantage in the council chamber than on the platform. Of his personal accomplishments during his thirty-five years of office, little can be said, for most of them were not evident. Not for him the hardships and the fierce joys of the pioneer carving out a new road; not for him the exhilaration and strain of constantly addressing large, expectant audiences. Wherever he went – and he traveled a great deal – his chief work was the same. Until the year of his retirement in 1935, his life was a continual round of interviews, committee meetings, office work, involving a degree of mental and spiritual concentration to which few attain. But his most effective service was the unremitting, watchful prayer that did not fluctuate nor slacken, whatever the strain of ill-health or work might be on him.

He came into office at a time when the work of the Mission was undergoing a complete change. It had never been Hudson Taylor's policy to secure a large number of converts in a short time by concentrated work in a limited area. Rather his plan had been to reach to the uttermost bounds of the great empire, establishing centers in strategic places in order that the gospel message might be carried far and wide. Now, after nearly forty years, the pioneer work was over. In all the provinces that had once been closed were mission stations – few and far between, in most cases, but nevertheless there. When Hudson Taylor died, there were over 10,000 members connected with the scattered churches. The foundations of the work had been laid. Now the time had come to build upon them.

Just how wonderfully God had worked can only be seen in retrospect. Truly the wrath of man does praise him! The Boxer Rising, which was planned to thrust foreign influence and the Christian religion out of China, had the final effect of opening up the country more than ever. The superior power of the Western nations was evident, and they must be appeased by treaties and trade concessions. Foreign trade increased, railways were opened, newspapers and periodicals, previously practically unknown, were published and sold throughout the country, and there was an entirely new attitude of respect towards foreigners. Everywhere opportunities for preaching and teaching abounded, and in the mission stations scattered throughout the country workers found themselves besieged by enquirers. The ground that had been ploughed and sown for so long at last showed signs of producing a plenteous harvest.

Mass movements commenced. These were first noticed in Szechwan, and then, through the ministry of such outstanding evangelists as Dr. Goforth of Manchuria, there were similar manifestations of the outpouring of the Holy Spirit in other provinces also. For some years these continued, and as one writer has said:

The work of grace of that period has left a lasting mark upon the work of God. The tide of worldliness within the church was stemmed; elements of strain, which had arisen in certain stations between the foreign and Chinese workers, were relieved; and the standard of holiness was raised. In short, the church in China was, as it were, born again, and brought to a realization of her place in the body of Christ.

Yet in all this stream of spiritual blessing, how carefully had the Mission to be steered lest it be carried away from fulfilling the purpose for which it had been brought into being! D. E. Hoste was far too wise a man not to be alive to the dangers, as well as the advantages, of the unprecedented opportunities of those days. He foresaw the possibility of missionaries being exploited by people who, under pretext of spiritual aims, would work for ends of their own. He was also apprehensive lest with the new demand for Western education the Mission should be diverted from the fulfilment of its commission of widespread evangelization and the building up of Chinese churches into the more limited channels of educational work.

Very early he had been impressed with the necessity for establishing a strong indigenous church with Chinese leadership. In all the many problems connected with the Mission which pressed in on him, he slowly but with determination steered towards this goal. Even in the Boxer Rising he saw an opportunity for placing greater responsibility on the Chinese church, and urged that this be done, though at that time there were very few who agreed with him. Now, as general director, he continually emphasized the necessity for the development of the gifts of Chinese Christians and their instruction in the Word of God. This was the keynote of his address at the first annual meeting he attended in London after the death of Hudson Taylor.

On the platform of the hall in which, twenty years previously, he had given his short, quiet testimony as a new missionary recruit, he now stood as the leader of the Mission. He wanted to make plain its present position in China to those at home upon whose interest and cooperation so much depended. Deeply conscious of his responsibility, he addressed his audience. With characteristic unemotional sincerity, he spoke:

> You are probably all aware that in earlier days the work of this Mission was almost entirely pioneering and itinerating in the various regions of inland China ... but that what we may call pastoral work in the nature of the case was not carried on, simply because there were no churches. Now, however, through God's blessing upon the labors of the missionaries, many districts, which years ago were the scenes of pioneering and itinerating work, have considerable numbers of Christians.
>
> This fact, of course, affects largely the work of the missionaries, and we find ourselves compelled to give attention to the instruction and training of converts.... We need your prayers, dear friends, for grace and wisdom and patience. So much will depend during the next twenty years upon our being able to instruct in the Word of God, and to instill into the churches correct standards of Christian life and Christian doctrine and practice. So much depends upon this, because the most superficial observer will see that the time is coming when China will be exposed to all the manifold influences of Western life. We shall have rationalism and secularism and all the varieties of spurious and false doctrine which abound in Christendom. These things will make their way into China, and unless we in the meantime have been able to raise up a generation of Christians grounded in the Word of God and established in sound doctrine, one cannot but tremble for the future of the church in China.
>
> And may I ask you as our fellow workers to pray that we may have grace in developing the gift and capacity of our Chinese fellow Christians. Let us remember that the Chinese as a people have accomplished a feat in the domain of government which has been unequalled by any other section of the human race.... The Chinese empire has held, as an organized corporate body, between two and three hundred million of people for many centuries.... We owe, I think, a tribute of respect to a race

which through many centuries has been able to govern such a vast number of people.

The point I want to make is this, that a people of this kind possess men capable of government on a large scale; and therefore we may expect to find, as time goes on, that the Spirit of the Lord will clothe himself with men who will be organizers and leaders of organizations of considerable magnitude.... Will you pray very much that the missionaries may have the grace and wisdom to make the most of their Chinese fellow workers, not to stunt them and stand in their way, but to help and strengthen them, and welcome them into fellowship in the care of the church as they are able to bear it.

In the years following the Boxer crisis institutional work took a larger place in the work of the Mission. Bible seminaries were started in different parts for the training of evangelists and pastors, while the number of schools increased, that young people might from their earliest years be instructed in the Word of God. Nevertheless, the vast majority of the members of the Mission continued in station work, evangelizing the areas for which they were responsible and teaching the converts. The foundations so faithfully laid by Hudson Taylor and the early workers were being built upon. In 1905, after forty years of missionary work, there were 12,000 baptized members of the China Inland Mission churches. By 1910 that number had been doubled, and by 1920 there were 52,000 in membership.

But D. E. Hoste desired something more than that mere numbers should be gathered into the church. "According to the grace of God which is given unto me, as a wise master builder, I have laid the foundation, and another buildeth thereon," wrote the apostle Paul. Hudson Taylor might have written the same words. Wisely indeed had he laid the foundations of his work in China! "But let every man take heed how he buildeth thereupon!" To D. E. Hoste was committed the task of building. Ever conscious of eternal values, he could not be deceived by an outward appearance of success. Of what quality was the church that was being built? In the day when every man's work shall be made manifest, how would it appear? Through the encouragements of the mass movements towards Christianity that began early in the century, through the perilous days of the Revolution in China, followed by the Great War in Europe, through years of financial pressure when trade slumps in the home countries had their inevitable effect of reducing support for foreign missions; the establishment of *a Chinese Church with Chinese leadership* was an aim never lost sight of in changing circumstances. A church must be built that would stand.

In the letters to fellow missionaries which occupied so important a place in his service, their relationship to Chinese colleagues, with this aim in view, was a constantly recurring theme.

> Shanghai
> November, 1914
>
> In early days, physical hardship and even danger were prominent features in the carrying on of our work. Whilst to a certain extent they still exist, it is true to say that trials and perplexities connected with the care of the growing Chinese churches bulk more largely in the experience of most of us. Now we need discernment and humility in order to adjust ourselves to changing conditions arising out of the growth of the Chinese ministry. To this end, we must in deed and in truth be men of prayer. It is only through spending much time in waiting upon God and in intercession that we shall ourselves obtain that wisdom and that spiritual influence which will enable us to pass safely through the present critical period in the development of the work. Do we take pains to acquaint ourselves with and to ponder the facts bearing upon the work entrusted to us? Hasty, ill-considered decisions, the outcome of mental indolence and rash carelessness, are more than ever to be guarded against now that the churches under our care are growing both in size and in intelligence. Again, the spirit that fails to recognize that others may be better qualified than ourselves for a particular work, and cannot stand aside and give them opportunity for taking it up, will not receive the divine blessing and guidance.

> Shanghai
> April, 1916
> Whilst there is much reason to be thankful for the large measure of good understanding and helpful cooperation which prevails between our Chinese fellow workers and ourselves, evidence is afforded in various parts of the field of the need of earnest prayer that these relationships may in all cases be maintained on a right basis. It is possible, sometimes through force of habit, to hold on to leadership and responsibility which could more helpfully be given to Chinese brethren; and we shall probably all feel our need of seeking for more love and discernment as we attempt to deal with these questions.

> Shanghai
> April, 1923
> Another cause for encouragement is the setting apart of a considerable number of pastors and other church officers; let us earnestly pray that those concerned may be helped in wisely entrusting real responsibility and leadership to these brethren. It is a truism to say that at the present time the growth and progress of the work largely depends upon right relationships and mutual adjustment of functions between the Chinese and foreign workers. Nothing is easier than to generalize upon this subject; few things are more difficult to work out in practice. Let us pray for divine grace and wisdom in dealing with it.

It was during a political upheaval, however, that D. E. Hoste's long-cherished ambition of a truly indigenous church began to take concrete form throughout the Mission. In 1927 anti-foreign feeling, which had been fermenting in China for some years, broke out with undisguised intensity. Not since 1900 had the position of missionaries been so perilous, and there was a wholesale withdrawal from the interior to the coast. In the disaster that seemed to many like the closing of the door for missionary work in China, he saw the opportunity for at least partial fulfillment of the vision granted nearly fifty years earlier. Meetings and discussions were arranged for the hundreds of workers who congregated at Shanghai, Chefoo, and other ports, and what was known as the new policy was formulated. Leadership in the churches for which the China Inland Mission was responsible was now to be vested in the Chinese themselves. The compulsory evacuation of missionaries from their stations made possible at a stroke a changeover which would otherwise have taken years to bring into effect. "Previous to the withdrawal from the field," he wrote in *China's Millions*, "considerable progress had been made in the establishment and building up of self-governing, self-supporting and self-propagating churches, which has always been one of our main objectives. After much prayer and also consultation with our fellow missionaries, we are convinced that a vigorous advance, with a view to the full realization of this objective, must now be made. In other words, there must be a full transfer of the oversight of the churches from the missionaries to the Chinese leaders.

"That greater liberty and independence will open the door to new dangers is evident. We are persuaded, however, that the worst evil is the stunting and even paralysis of Chinese leadership by undue continuance of the missionary's oversight."

When the turn of the tide came, and the country was sufficiently freed from disorderly elements to allow Westerners to live in the interior again, missionaries returned to enter upon a new phase of their work. Difficulties and problems awaited them, no less discouraging because they were of a different order from those of the past. The general director knew too much about spiritual warfare to be taken by surprise that this fresh advance was not uncontested. But the advance had been made. Some of the land for which the pioneers had given their lives had been possessed. An indigenous church that could stand alone was being built.

As the Mission grew, it took increasingly an acknowledged place amongst the denominational missionary societies working in China. In the early pioneering days, it had been alone – an organism, largely composed of laymen, called into being by God for the opening up of inland China to the gospel. With the passing of the years and the entry of denominational societies into the field it was not always easy for the missionaries of the China Inland Mission to accept the peculiar position in which they stood as members of a body which claimed no backing from any recognized ecclesiastical body, particularly when the standing of the Mission and its members were criticized! At one period a number felt themselves to be under a disadvantage because of their lack of formal ordination, and the matter had to be thrashed out in the China council. How many and far-reaching were the results of those council meetings! How easily might the usefulness and direction of the whole Mission have been hampered or deflected by a wrong decision made in the quiet of the council chamber!

On this occasion the matter was looked at from every angle, and one point stood out clearly. In the minutes it was recorded: "In the course of the discussion it was brought out that one important reason which led the founder of the Mission to start the work was to provide an outlet for the type of worker that the denominational societies were not prepared to receive; hence, any measure which tended to infringe or gradually to alter this fundamental feature of the Mission should be guarded against. Nor was it desirable that the membership of the Mission should become divided into two divisions of clerical and lay workers, one enjoying a supposedly higher status than the other. It was to be feared that as time went on, under such an order of things, the very class of worker which in the first instance it was intended to send to China should come to be rejected as unsuitable."

The Mission had a contribution to make different from that of the denominational societies. It was "a solely missionary organization," not a denomination, and this individuality must be preserved. Even if for the sake of the work, ordination was in some cases advisable; the Mission as a body must maintain its inter-denominational character, and its members, whether ordained or not, would be on an equal basis, and classified simply as "missionaries."

In the important matter of accepting candidates, D. E. Hoste continually emphasized that educational and social advantages were not to be regarded as being of primary importance. The vital thing was that the men and women sent to China should know the power of prayer, and exercise it, be approved by their brethren, and know they were called of God to serve him in China.

> Few things are more remarkable about the Judges of Israel than the wide variety of types of men represented by them. Drawn from different tribes and from widely different positions in life, they were, both in personality, previous experience, and training, as varied a company as can well be imagined. The lesson is thus emphasized of the importance of keeping an open mind and a wide view in estimating the qualifications of those claiming to be called to special service. There is need of constant prayer and watchfulness against the tendency insensibly to become narrow and stereotyped in our judgment of men, weighing them in balances in some respects more in accord with our own prepossessions than with those laid down in the Scriptures.

. . . .

The editor of the leading English newspaper in China once interviewed the general director of the China Inland Mission, and the subject of leadership was introduced.

> Mr. Hoste was extremely interesting on the subject of the qualities which enable a man to rule and lead his fellows," he wrote. "I believe in an aristocracy," said Mr. Hoste. "But a man is an aristocrat not because his grandfather was before him, but by his own powers." He went on to speak of two men whom he had known in the Mission, the one born in high places with every advantage, the other in lowly, and with none. But there could be no question which of them was the one to bear rule. And Mr. Hoste added a curious piece of information; that to have been an artisan, to have worked with one's hands, appears often to be some of the best preparation to teach a man to understand and lead his fellows. So he would remove all artificial disabilities; he would have all men start from scratch. The aristocracy will not fail to appear.

CHAPTER Nine

Spiritual Leadership

NEARLY thirty years had elapsed since Hoste had first shouldered the responsibility that told so heavily upon him. It is probably true to say that the greatest burden of his work was the consciousness that upon him, humanly speaking, devolved the direction of the lives of his fellow missionaries. He was asked once if he was worried about Mission finances. It would not have been altogether surprising to learn that he was; but he shook his head. There had been too many evidences of God's care for the material needs of his servants to warrant anxiety on that score.

"No," he answered; "not particularly. *Men and women are much more difficult to get and to handle than money."* The handling of men and women, creatures of flesh and blood like himself, with their human frailties and emotions, their possibilities and limitations – this was what told on him."

"As general director of the China Inland Mission," wrote Dr. Kitchen, for many years home director of the work in Australasia, "he realized the responsibility of his position so keenly and to such a degree that if there was any failure in any part of the Mission, he almost felt that he himself had been negligent and was in some way blameworthy. This led him to spend the hours he did in intercessory prayer."

It was his prayer life on behalf of the Mission that impressed those who knew him more than anything else, for intercession for his fellow missionaries was regarded as his first duty towards them, and was put before everything. Those who worked in the administration offices all knew his procedure. Punctually he would walk into his office in the morning and glance through the pile of letters awaiting his attention. If he saw any he knew to be urgent, or of special importance, he would open and read them. Otherwise, they were left unopened on the desk. The door was closed, and a card marked "Engaged" indicated he was not to be disturbed. Inside the room two people knelt to pray, for D. E. Hoste almost invariably invited someone to be with him for this ministry. Sometimes his wife joined him; sometimes he would invite a member of the staff or a missionary passing through Shanghai; for he found the presence of another kept his mind from wandering.

"Before the work of intercession began, there was a period of worship, when he knelt by his chair and entered into the holiest of all by virtue of the precious blood," wrote one who acted as his secretary for a time. "The language of adoration and worship used is too sacred to be written about. Then began the work of intercession, when station after station, worker after worker was brought to the Lord in loving remembrance."

He spent much time in prayer before coming to decisions about matters concerning individual missionaries and administration.

"I do envy those people who seem to get guidance about important matters so easily!" he said more than once. "I often have to pray and pray and wait and wait before I get my guidance!"

His knowledge of the personnel of the Mission was extraordinary. When there were over 1,200 members and associates, he knew each one by name, where each one was working, the difficulties of the work in which each was engaged. Chinese leaders and fellow workers were also remembered. And he knew the names of all the children of the Mission! During the War of 1914-18 he visited England, and found on arrival at the Mission home in Newington Green that the sons of missionaries in the fighting forces were prayed for regularly. When he saw the list, however, he was not satisfied.

"But where," he enquired, "are the sons of our German brethren?"

They had not been mentioned by name in prayer – only collectively. Indeed, it is doubtful whether anyone could have supplied the names of them all. Twenty-four hours later, however, they were added. The general director knew the names of the children of the Continental Associate workers by heart!

D. E. Hoste's ministry of prayer was no easy expression of mere emotion, nor was it a lifeless formula. "He always maintained that prayer was work," wrote James Stark, who was secretary of the Mission in Shanghai for practically the whole period of D.E. Hoste's directorship, "and like Epaphras he knew what it was to labor fervently in prayer for others, sometimes with fasting. On his own confession, he often found that this sacred exercise involved spiritual conflict."

Some of those who shared his periods of intercession got a glimpse into the strain they imposed on him. In 1925, in a weakened state of health, he was traveling to Australia, and the one who accompanied him wrote:

> Intercessory prayer was a tremendous physical exercise to him – a wrestling with "the powers of darkness." One morning, a few days before he would recognize that he was really ill, during our time of intercession, he simply wrestled in prayer, and cried to the Lord in agony to deliver poor China from the awful power of demons and principalities and powers, and he quite broke down and burst into tears – the only time I ever saw him weep. He could not possibly stand this strain when he was so ill, and was not able to maintain our daily periods of united prayer and intercession; but I have no doubt that he spent much time in silent prayer.

About this conscious conflict with wicked spirits he spoke very little. There are indeed few who know anything about it in its awful reality who care to discuss it. Easy talk on the subject is usually the fruit of shallow experience. D. E. Hoste referred but rarely to the unseen forces against which he was called to wage war, but he was constantly aware of them; and behind failures on the part of missionaries, who are, after all, but "men of like passions with ourselves," he saw the activity of the powers of evil. He wrote:

> It must be remembered that there are "spiritual wickednesses" at the back of all confusion and discord in the work of God. The servant of Christ must, therefore, practically recognize that his warfare is with these satanic beings and must be waged on his knees. In no other way can any one of us be used by God to deal effectively with troubles in his church. There must be persevering prayer and intercession before the powers of darkness are driven back. How blessed that this great truth lays it open to the weakest of us to prevail in matters which would otherwise be entirely beyond our strength and wisdom.
>
> It is far more difficult to continue steadfastly in intercession on behalf of those amongst whom we are called to minister than to engage in outward activities for their good. And yet, if the powers of darkness, which are blinding the minds of men and hindering the work of God, are not overcome through sacrificial prayer, little, if anything, is really accomplished.
>
> I have found that waiting upon God and intercession on behalf of others, are really the most vital and effective parts of my service. You will remember the stress placed upon this in the Scripture, and also one or two figures of speech indicating that it is often attended with difficulty and suffering, due in part, at any rate, to the persistent opposition of the powers of darkness, who can only be overcome by perseverance and importunity in prayer.

He had developed to a marked degree an appreciative discernment of the gifts of others and a patient, impartial penetration of mind which saw to the heart of things. This natural ability was recognized by his colleagues. What affected them far more, however, was the knowledge of his intense, real, and sustained prayer life. They all knew that any decisions made concerning them had been arrived at only after much prayer; and for this reason, perhaps more than any other, they were willing to accept appointments from which they themselves shrank. And how often at the Saturday evening prayer meetings in Shanghai, when missionaries visiting headquarters gave their testimonies, were confessions made that the designations which had appeared to be wrong had after all proved to be right!

"He was our director, and he directed us," it was said long years afterwards, "and the outcome of his work is to be judged by the ministry of those he directed. He sent Edgar to the Tibetans, Fraser to the tribes, Mather to Sinkiang, and hundreds of us to less-known spheres of labor; and he sent us to the right places!"

He himself had a clear apprehension of the type of leadership required of him.

> My personal judgment, for what it may be worth, is that capacity to appreciate the gifts and powers of widely varying kinds of workers, and then to help them along the lines of their own personalities and working, is the main quality for oversight in a Mission like ours.

In his dealings with missionaries and their problems, he always took pains to ascertain all the facts of a case before arriving at a decision. Writing once to a colleague in the homelands, he said:

> In practice, perhaps the most vitally important matter for those who are leaders is to be most patient and careful in ascertaining by comprehensive enquiry from different groups the actual facts of a given situation before pronouncing any opinion, much less taking any action. As the Scripture says, "He that judgeth a matter before he hears it, it shall be shame and folly unto him." Few things encourage the deadly practice of tale-bearing more than for anyone in a leading position to be known as willing to listen to it – it may be, even desirous to hear it – and then without enquiring of those concerned to write foolish, crude warnings and reproofs, the only effect of which is to injure his own influence and standing with those whom he has hastily and unjustly condemned.

In the council chamber, where decisions affecting the whole life and work of the Mission were made, this same slowness to arrive at a decision was evident. When matters of importance were being discussed, he invariably waited until all had spoken, and every aspect of the case dealt with, before he gave his own opinion. It often happened that although many helpful suggestions had been made, there was a lack of unanimity in the idea put forward. The general director would then speak, and with tact and courtesy uniting and incorporating the various suggestions, arrive at a conclusion which won everyone's approval. He worked by cooperation – he directed, rather than dictated. He did not win the confidence and respect of his colleagues by chance, but by the careful and studied observance of natural and spiritual laws. He wrote:

> Colleagueship calls for an orientation and method different from the direct rule over juniors and subordinates. Capacity to recognize and assimilate what is sound and helpful from important men and, at least in part and with modifications, to apply it, seems to be a more difficult and complex matter.
>
> I feel more and more that it is a mistake to suppose that different personalities from one's own which have the defects of their qualities do not possess also positive requirements, both as to insight and expression, in which I myself am lacking.
>
> If we give our confidence to our fellow workers, Chinese and foreign, they will give us theirs; on the other hand, a mistrustful, grudging spirit begets a like attitude in those around us. Again, if we are open to the influences and opinions of our companions, they will be so towards ours. Force of habit and egotism, more or less unconscious at times, may lead us to overestimate our own powers and undervalue those of others, and so to prevent the latter from freely exercising their gifts. Such a course, persisted in, often leads to a rude awakening to the fact that our own ministry is not wanted.
>
> There is need of constant prayer and watchfulness against the tendency insensibly to become narrow and stereotyped in our judgment of men, weighing them in balances in some

respects more in accord with our own prepossessions than with those laid down in the Scriptures.

It was his sincere appreciation of the qualities and gifts of others which won him the confidence and respect of men of other nations whose traditions and temperaments were often entirely different from his own.

"Mr. Hoste was a student of men, and possessed the gift of discernment in large measure," wrote one who traveled with him to the home centers of Continental missionary societies associated with the China Inland Mission. "The German thoroughness, the Scandinavian graciousness, the simplicity or the subtlety of different minds were recognized, while the sensibilities of national outlook were never intentionally offended. But the real success of Mr. Hoste's relationship with the Continental fellow workers was his sincere and deep appreciation of the reality of their faith and the self-sacrifice of their lives. This appreciation cannot be simulated."

Sincere appreciation of the virtues and talents of others, however, is not sufficient to achieve and maintain unity. In the long run, loyalty is perhaps an even more indispensable quality. As a colleague, D. E. Hoste was entirely trustworthy. "He was one who would never betray confidences," it was said of him; neither was he willing to listen to criticisms or tale-bearing. He wrote:

> Whilst recognizing the abstract right of our brethren, and in some circumstances their duty, to discuss and criticize arrangements either here or at home, as a rule I doubt the benefit of the practice. I need hardly say that references of that kind about home centers are sometimes made by returning workers. Not very long ago, for instance, someone from ——— told me he thought there were several matters there calling for improvement. I purposely made no answer, feeling if they were important he would mention them. He kept silent, so the subject dropped, and I do not know what he meant. My rule is not to respond to such remarks, my feeling being that the good feeling and true fellowship between national centers is likely

to be impaired thereby. Such has been my experience. Definite complaints from returning workers will receive attention; but I think to countenance criticism does not, as a rule, tend to promote unity; rather the reverse.

"How much harm can be done by 'the talk of the lips,'" he wrote on another occasion, "in unguarded, ill-advised discussion by the Lord's people, of his work and workers!

"Looking back over these fifty years, I really think that if I were asked to mention one thing which has done more harm and occasioned more sorrow and division in God's work than anything else, I should say tale-bearing."

He had a wonderful insight into character. On an amazingly short acquaintance he could form an accurate estimate of a person's character, ability, and qualifications. But perhaps his outstanding gift was his statesmanship. He viewed things as from a mountain-top, never being confused by immediate issues, but seeing right through to their ultimate conclusion. It was this faculty more than any other that won for him a reputation that spread far beyond the region of his own jurisdiction. That the leaders of other missions frequently sought his counsel was no secret. With a mind that was never baffled by the complexities of a situation, nor sidetracked by them, he had a simple directness which was sometimes almost disconcerting.

In a large hall in Shanghai a conference of the representatives of the leading Protestant missions in China was in progress. The question of qualifications for leadership was being discussed. As the debate continued, one and another speaking vigorously and at some length, D. E. Hoste sat quietly listening. Many glances were cast in his direction, but he remained silent until at last the chairman turned to him and asked if he had anything to say on the subject.

From all over the hall came murmurs of approval at the invitation. Here was one they wanted to hear! His contributions to a discussion were always listened to with more than ordinary interest.

There was a slight pause; and then, as the slim, erect figure arose, a hush fell on the assembly. What had the leader of the mission which had more workers on the field than any other Protestant society in China to say? What did he consider was the proof of a man's fitness for leadership? All eyes turned to him now – but it is doubtful if any caught a twinkle in his eye as he made his reply.

"It occurs to me," he said in his curious, high-pitched voice, "that perhaps the best test of whether one is a qualified leader is to find out whether anyone is following him!"

Chapter Ten

The Man Himself

Up and down a shady path in the quiet Shanghai compound of the China Inland Mission walked the general director. People came and went across the lawns or walked along the wide, arched veranda of the home and headquarters offices, but no one approached him. It was understood that he must not be disturbed. He walked up and down alone, his lips moving in silent prayer, laying the burdens of his soul upon the only one who could bear them for him.

A child wandered over and looked at him rather wistfully. Her mother had told her she must not disturb Mr. Hoste, so she dared not go too near or say anything. Like most children, however, she was unaccountably drawn to this man of whom older people were often rather afraid; and when he saw her and held out his hand, she ran forward instinctively to slip her own into it. The warm, confiding touch of her little hand in his gave a sense of release to his spirit; and as he continued to walk up and down, prayer flowed on in a steady stream, while the child trotted quietly and contentedly beside him. She was about five, and he was nearly fifty, but what did that matter? They trusted each other; and as he poured out his heart in intercession for matters far beyond her understanding and interest, she heard her own name mentioned.

"Mr. Hoste prayed for me this morning!" she announced when she returned to her mother. And when she was rebuked for bothering him, she said in simple self-justification, "But he held out his hand!"

He was fond of children, especially little girls, but he was not in any sense what could be termed a "family man." By birth and upbringing, he was a soldier, and a soldier he remained. His early training had impressed upon him the military principle of putting duty to king and country before every other claim; and when he was called to engage in a higher warfare than that of his forefathers, the same principle dominated his service.

He may be said to have had no real family life all the time he was general director. He and his wife had a small private sitting room, but mealtimes always found him in his accustomed place at the long table in the dining room of the Mission home; and even when his sons returned for their school holidays, there was not much privacy for the general director and his family. Indeed, his children saw very little of him when they were young, for he traveled much during his long years of office and was frequently away from home. One of his sons said that though while a boy he had little opportunity to know D. E. Hoste as a father, in later years he came to know him as a friend. "He was a *good friend!*" he added warmly. In that relationship he excelled.

He never forgot that he had once been a soldier, and that memory sometimes filled him with an ingenuous boyish pride. A missionary who had gone to him for discussion and prayer was surprised when, on hearing the strains of a military band as it passed by along the street outside, the general director suddenly tapped his shoulder and said, "I used to belong to that!"

There was an originality about his prayer habits which was sometimes almost disconcerting. In the midst of his intercessions he would suddenly stop, cross to his desk and make a note or two about something that had occurred to him, and then continue walking about, praying. After such a pause, however, he would occasionally turn to whoever was with him and ask, "Where had I got to?" When a mid-morning cup of tea or cocoa was brought to him, he would courteously accept it, and as likely as not pour half of it into the saucer, hand it to his companion with a murmured apology, and go on praying, taking occasional sips from his cup meanwhile! Prayer to him was as natural as a child talking to a father whose perfect love had cast out all fear.

Consistent self-denial characterized his personal life. No

"subtle love of softening things" was permitted to weaken him. He knew how much the success of a campaign depends on the vigilance and self-control of the one who is the leader. Even in small matters he kept strict watch over himself. Although he had a very "sweet tooth," his wife knew it would be useless to buy him cakes – only if they had guests to tea in their little private sitting room would he partake. When they were alone he refused to indulge his taste, for he begrudged the money spent on himself.

His sense of stewardship was very keen. The recipient from time to time of considerable sums of money, he did not accept them lightly as being for his own personal use. He received one substantial legacy which, after a day of prayer and fasting, he donated entirely to the Mission. Although he and his wife continued to live in simplicity, the burdens of many in financial difficulties were lightened by their gifts. Their generosity to others was unstinting. Missionaries who happened to celebrate their birthdays in Shanghai always received a present from the general director and his wife.

He was a man of deep understanding and sympathy, particularly where young missionaries were concerned. Not a few, facing some unforeseen problem in their early days on the mission field, found the outwardly aloof, rather stern general director an unexpected ally and a wise counsellor. In the many affairs of wide importance that so constantly occupied his mind, he always had time for new workers, and their letters received his personal attention.

"I could go to him with all my problems," said one who, as a young missionary, had sometimes been perplexed about the attitude she should adopt towards some of the intricate problems of the mission field. "He always knew what was the right course, and *could tell me the reason why.*"

J. O. Fraser, of Lisuland, was asked, after his first furlough, to act as D. E. Hoste's secretary for a while. Young, strong, mentally alert, in a letter home he gave a vivid little pen picture of his leader:

Mr. Hoste is a very fine man, and it was a tremendous privilege to me to have so much time with him. He is only sixty-three, but has had such a wearing life that he looks much older. He is what you would call an old-fashioned English gentleman with a little touch of formality and precision running all through his humor, genuine kindness, and humble spirit. He would be in his element in the society of men of affairs and men of learning, but he has voluntarily come amongst us people of lower stature – above whom he stands head and shoulders. He has read widely and his special hobby is the study of human nature, whether in books or in real life. After several hours spent in prayer every morning, he will go for a walk and turn his mind into entirely different channels, discussing with you the character of the Prince Consort, Dr. Johnson, the Duke of Wellington and all sorts of other people, ancient and modern. Or he will tell you of men he has met and generalize on different types, classes, races, etc. He is a tremendously keen observer, and seems to retain all he reads and sees. He is a stern self-disciplinarian and insists on the necessity for discipline in everything.

A certain austerity of manner makes him feared by some, but he is the kindest and gentlest of men at heart. We had arguments over all sorts of things. I told him that I did not believe he liked children. He insisted that he did – "I assure you that I do, Mr. Fraser, but I could not stand their noise." He is so nerve-tired at present that one counts it a privilege to protect him in all sorts of ways. He was kind enough to tell me that my companionship had made all the difference to his stay at Kuling.

I could write a small book about Mr. Hoste. Beside the tremendous respect I have for him, and admiration, he fills a special place in my life, and has done for years, as a kind of spiritual father.

It is perhaps inevitable that a leader will often be misunderstood. His responsibility it is to make decisions and take action which to the imperfectly informed seem unreasonable, and he is often blamed for things over which he himself has no control.

That D. E. Hoste often knew the bitterness of that experience there can be no doubt; and while he endured it without attempting to justify himself, he nevertheless felt it, and to some of his intimates confided how hurt he had been sometimes.

One misty day, while staying at the Mission's holiday home on the hill resort of Kuling, he rather solemnly asked to have a private word with the host and hostess after morning prayers. Everyone else quickly left the room, and D. E. Hoste confronted the couple before him.

"Don't you think we have had enough of this?" he asked. "I really think it is up to you people to do better for us!"

His hostess looked puzzled and anxious. What was wrong? What did he mean? An inveterate tease, he enjoyed their questioning looks, and did not elucidate his remark immediately! It seemed as though he was really unsatisfied with their service.

"Well," he said at last, "we've had this mist up here for three days now!"

"Oh, Mr. Hoste!" exclaimed the wife, relieved that there was nothing wrong after all, while her husband simply smiled. Delighted with his joke, D. E. Hoste smiled, too. But before he turned away he said quietly:

"That's no worse than I get! I'm often blamed for things I can no more help than you can help this mist!"

Willingness to accept blame in order that others may be shielded is a rare quality. The desire to justify oneself in the eyes of one's fellows is deep-rooted in human nature, and it is not easy to be misjudged and remain silent. The quiet majesty of Christ is perhaps nowhere seen to better advantage than on the occasion when, being accused of many things, he answered not a word. Those who will follow him sometimes find themselves in positions in which they must adopt a like attitude.

On one occasion an arrangement was made in which a missionary found himself in circumstances distasteful to him, and which were, in fact, rather unjust. He attributed the arrangement to D. E. Hoste, whereas actually it was due to the inadvertent action of his fellow missionary. The general director heard, later on, how he had been misunderstood; and it was suggested that he should clear himself in the eyes of the missionary concerned.

"No," he said thoughtfully. "Let it stand as it is. Better that he should think it is me than that it should come between the two of them in their work."

Although the nature of his service was administrative rather than evangelistic, he never lost his love for souls nor his sense of personal responsibility for those who knew not Christ. Every day he went for a walk through the streets of Shanghai – down to the Bund, along by the racecourse, or over towards the French Concession. Often, during the football and cricket seasons, he went to the playing fields, watching the games with intense delight. Oppressed by a day of heavy work in the office, it was a relief to get out and turn his mind away from the matters that had been claiming his attention. Too mentally tired for much preaching or personal work, however, he still grasped at opportunities for making the gospel known. In his hand was a little bundle of tracts, and he would pause every now and then in his walk to give one away, courteously raising his hat as he did so.

There were some who considered this humble form of evangelism rather mechanical.

"Well," said D. E. Hoste, "to my mind it is better than doing nothing! I pray over this ministry to the people." On his journeys to mission stations in the interior he invariably carried tracts, and those who traveled with him observed that he was "always on the job."

The wideness of his prayer-interest was extraordinary. While China naturally claimed most of his attention, he followed the work of missions in other parts of the world with the keenest interest. On one occasion he amazed the people who were attending a prayer meeting by his intercessions for Africa. He prayed all over the continent, geographically, mentioning mission after mission, station after station, worker after worker, revealing a deep understanding of the different problems confronting the missionaries. This knowledge of other mission fields was equally extensive. He had once heard D. L. Moody speak on the verse,

"Lift up your eyes, and look on the fields," and it made an impression upon him that he never forgot. In his practical way he took the divine injunction to mean that he should obtain all the information he could about God's work in every land and support it by his intercessions. Throughout his life he continued to do this.

It is perhaps surprising that next to his prayerfulness D. E. Hoste's strangely puckish sense of humor made the deepest impression on those who knew him. Without the trace of a smile on his face he would pass a remark or ask a question which would cause surprise and embarrassment to the unhappy object of his wit! Those who could take his fun in good part, without getting either offended or afraid of him, won his admiration.

He took an impish delight in playing with the small children of fellow missionaries and telling him that his name was "Old Hoste."

"Who am I, now?" he would question them. "Old Hoste," was the innocent reply. But picture the confusion of the mother who, knowing nothing of the private instruction her child had received from the general director, was horrified when the little one, seeing him sitting in the dining room, announced, "There's Old Hoste!"

Both he and his wife had poor health. He suffered from sprue and anemia, while she for years was more or less confined to her room, a semi-invalid. Her strength was very limited and easily overtaxed, with the result that she had severe headaches and suffered from insomnia, besides having gastric trouble. It was a trial to both of them that she should suffer in this way, especially as it meant she was often unable to take her place beside him.

An affectionate husband, he frequently referred to the help she was to him. "She is beyond praise," he said once; while on another occasion he raised a laugh when he lugubriously admitted that his wedding day was not the happiest day of his life – it had been getting happier ever since! Nevertheless, he was "a man's man." He enjoyed the society of his own sex, and on the not infrequent occasions when nerve-tiredness necessitated his taking a short holiday, he reveled in walks and talks with a man companion. Gradually, as the strain of a mind over-pressed with responsibility was eased, he became lighthearted and friendly, and would sometimes even talk a little about himself. When he returned to his work, however, the old reserve reasserted itself. Appreciative of companionship and sympathy though he was, his position as leader and his own inherent reserve to a great extent separated him from others; and while he was courteous to all and friendly with a few, it is probably true to say that he was intimate with none. Down through the years that brought much of strain and anxiety, aging him prematurely, the general director walked alone.

• • • • •

"The *pressure*!"

D. E. Hoste was talking to Mrs. Howard Taylor. The subject of their conversation was the book she had written on the life of Hudson Taylor. Just once or twice, however, there came a glimpse into his own life.

"The pressure!" he said. "It goes on from stage to stage, pressed beyond measure, every true work of God. It changes with every period of your life. The most killing years of my life were 1904, 1905, 1906 – terrible! The pressure of the *work*. I was half-killed! One has been able to make arrangements since then. There is less strain of work now, but other things develop. He eases you at one end, brings you into new things at the other...."

"The pressure." It does not speak of an easy life, or one that was free from care. At one time the floods of a personal anxiety and grief threatened to engulf him to such an extent that he seriously contemplated resigning from his position. "Pressed beyond measure – cast down, but not forsaken"; such phrases present no pictures of those who walk straight through every trial or difficulty as though they did not exist! Neither are they applicable to those who walk under cloudless skies with the happy confidence of treading an assured pathway. D. E. Hoste once admitted that when he was young he seemed to "walk under an open heaven";

prayers were answered quickly; guidance was easily obtained. But now it was not so. Often he felt like a man in the dark, scarcely able to see the next step ahead.

"I more and more see," he wrote in 1926, "that as we go on in the Christian life the Lord very often does not want to give us the sense of his presence or the consciousness of help. There again Mr. Taylor helped me very much. We were talking about guidance. He said how in his younger life things used to come so clearly, so quickly, to him. 'But,' he said, 'now as I have gone on and God has used me more and more I seem often to be like a man going along in a fog. I do not know what to do.' Of course, as you get older and the wear and tear of things tells upon you, you are rather like that sometimes. Naturally, people vary.

"The Lord loves a man who trusts him. That is all he wants. Be willing to say, 'I am a poor little miserable thing, nothing,' and then, if people walk over you, never mind. They walked over Jesus the Son of God, and put him on the cross, and he was obedient.

"Get the gospel right into your heart; receive it, and believe it. Do not think that you can mend matters with your efforts. I used to talk to people and say, 'You must be humble. You must try to live lovingly one with another. You must try to adapt yourself to the Chinese. Be diligent, and do not get lazy.' Well, those things all have their place. But I believe, for myself, and so I pass it on to other people, that we must trust. That is all you can do, and all he wants you to do."

As the years passed, this attitude of quiet confidence in God deepened. "Trust" was a word he used constantly. Speaking to a group of Cambridge men once, he told them that this lesson of trusting in God for daily living was the lesson of greatest importance he had learned, and which he saw to be of chief importance for the Christian.

"We talk about learning new lessons; but really, it is just learning the same old lesson, 'Trust him,' deeper down!"

Chapter Eleven

The Forward Movement

NINE men sat round the oblong table in the director's office, pouring over a map of China. They were of varying ages, drawn from different walks of life, each with his own individuality and temperament and gifts. Yet from D. E. Hoste, approaching his seventieth year, to J. O. Fraser, the youngest member of the council, all were united in heart as they concentrated on the matter under consideration. China! China with her four hundred and fifty million people; China with her ten million Moslems; China with her various tribes scattered over the grassy uplands of Tibet, the rugged mountains of the southwest, the wild wastes of Chinese Turkestan. To the evangelization of China they had early consecrated their lives. China's need of Christ they could never forget. They were gathered now to view the land that yet remained to be possessed – the land over which the feet of them that bring glad tidings of good things had not yet passed, and to consider how best to commence to possess it.

It was during the conferences held in 1927, the year of evacuation, that the seed of the Forward Movement was sown. As the missionaries were detained month after month at the coast, another subject besides that of placing church responsibility on the Chinese leaders forced itself upon them. It was a time of heart-searching as the return to the interior continued to be delayed, and the questions they began to ask themselves were these:

"Is the C.I.M. actually doing the work for which God brought it into being? Have we too readily settled down to the task of consolidating gains already secured, while multitudes of people remain unevangelized and great stretches of country are unoccupied for Christ? Are we not in danger of becoming 'stationary' instead of mobile? Are we too much occupied with the near at hand? Have we lost the vision of those afar off and still unreached?"

At a meeting of over one hundred missionaries, therefore, it was resolved:

> That the Mission be urged definitely to pray and plan for a big Forward Movement, with a view to a fulfilment of its responsibility for the evangelization of the Chinese, Mohammedans, Tribes, Tibetans, and others in the field allotted to it. That this Forward Movement include:
>
> (a) The speedy and thorough evangelization of all walled cities and of other strategic points in all fields now recognized as being within the sphere of C.I.M. work.
>
> (b) A well-planned attack upon the strongholds of Islam, particularly in Kansu and Sinkiang.
>
> (c) A systematic designation of workers to occupy all strategic points in the Tribes area, ensuring the evangelization of all unreached Tribes.
>
> (d) The extension of work for Tibet and Mongolia.

And the last clause in the resolution read:

"Resolved, that we seek the prayerful fellowship, counsel, judgment and cooperation of the Chinese church with us in carrying out this Forward Movement." What a note of unconscious triumph in that clause! What as but an almost unbelievable dream fifty years ago was a reality now. There was a Chinese church to reckon on!

Meanwhile, the Spirit of God was stirring at home. It was a time when retrenchment in missionary work in China seemed inevitable to many, and there was an atmosphere of depression abroad which was a challenge to faith. In the London headquarters of the Mission the conviction was born that the Lord wanted them to take a new step forward – now, when trade slumps at home and the situation in China itself seemed to indicate that a Forward Movement was an impossibility!

The urge to reach those who were still beyond the range of the witnesses of the gospel was growing. The increased responsibility being placed upon Chinese church leaders would inevitably set free a number of missionaries for a further movement forward. In September, 1928, in the little office in Shanghai that served as a council chamber, a statement of policy was formulated, which dealt mainly with the various questions arising out of the handing over of church responsibility to Chinese leaders. In that statement, however, appeared the words:

"In view of the many cities and great tracts of country still unevangelized in the spheres for which the C.I.M. is considered responsible, we believe that the time has come for more definite effort to secure the evangelization of our whole field." And now, in March 1929, the nine men were gathered to view the vast field for which the Mission accepted responsibility. D. E. Hoste rose to his feet to give a report on the populations of the areas under review, and the missionary work (so pathetically inadequate) already existing in them. In each one of the provinces which sixty years previously had so burdened the heart of Hudson Taylor, not only were missionaries working, but churches had been established. Yet how great was the task still to be accomplished! How many millions were still passing into eternity every year without once having heard the name of Jesus!

The province of Chinese Turkestan, far away in the northwest, bordering Tibet and Mongolia, came in for special discussion. For years George Hunter had labored there alone. Now he had Percy Mather, a younger worker, with him; while a trio of intrepid women, Eva and Francesca French and Mildred Cable, were taking long itinerant journeys across the great stretches of the Gobi Desert. Yet how inadequate a force that was for a population of two or three million people, comprising a dozen different racial groups, scattered over an area stretching as far as from Shanghai to the border of Tibet – the breadth of China!

Yet the clamant needs of China proper could not be lost sight of in the contemplation of the more distant and sparsely populated areas. As they looked at the map and viewed, as it were, great tracts of country in which lived millions of people who had not heard the gospel, in spite of missionary occupation for over half a century, they realized anew the greatness of the task which still remained unfinished. The burden of responsibility for those who knew not the name whereby alone men can be saved could not be shelved. D. E. Hoste felt his heart stirred anew with the consuming passion of his youth. "If this gospel is true," he had thought then, "and I know it is, as it has changed my life – I want to make it known where Christ is not known. There are many people in other lands who have never heard it, and the Lord wants them to hear it, for he says so. I want to give my life to this."

"I want to give my life to this." He knew by this time what giving his life to it meant. He knew as few did the fierceness of spiritual conflict; the long hours of travailing in prayer; the mind constantly pressed with a sense of responsibility for workers on the field. Physical privation and hardship is not the only price to be paid that the people who have never heard shall hear. He was soon to enter his seventieth year, the age at which workers in the Mission were due to retire. Was this the time for a new effort?

Other sheep have I which are not of this fold: them also I must bring.

I must *bring* ...

There is a certain type of emotion that goes too deep for words and gets no relief from outbursts of enthusiasm. Only action which accomplishes can give satisfaction. As he, with the China council, considered the field, he knew that something must be done.

A sub-committee was appointed to make an estimate of the number of new workers that would be required to begin a further movement forward, and they came back with the report that one hundred and ninety-nine were needed!

Similar surveys had been made in the past. When Hudson Taylor, in 1865, prayed for twenty-four willing, skillful workers, it was with a definite and specific plan in mind. Years later the field was reviewed, and the possibility of another ordered advance was seen, with the result that an appeal went out, this time for seventy new workers. The seventy were forthcoming, and at a still later period *one hundred recruits* were asked for – and received!

But those mountain peaks were reached during the last century, at a time of prosperity in the Western nations, and in the case of the hundred, during a spiritual revival following the far-reaching and lasting effects of Moody's ministry. The situation was different now. The War of 1914-18 had resulted in economic depression from which the nations involved were only just recovering, while spiritually there was no movement comparable with that experienced in the latter part of the nineteenth century. Was this the time to expect response to an appeal for such a number of workers as were now seen to be necessary? Two things remained unchanged, however: the need of the millions who were still dying without the knowledge of Christ, and the faithfulness of the God who answers prayer offered in the name of Jesus. Together the council read through a letter written when the appeal for seventy new missionaries was sent out by Hudson Taylor and his colleagues in 1883.

"Souls on every hand are perishing for lack of knowledge," they read. "More than a thousand every hour is passing away into death and darkness. We, and many others, have been sent by God and by the churches to minister the bread of life to these perishing ones; but our number collectively is utterly inadequate to the crying needs around us. Provinces in China compare in area with kingdoms in Europe, and average between ten and twenty million in population ... and none are sufficiently supplied with laborers. Can we leave matters thus without incurring the sin of bloodguiltiness?"

Nearly fifty years had passed since those words were written, yet they seemed as potent now as then. The Spirit who had animated the early pioneers of the Mission was still urging forward;

and the nine men gathered around the table could not but obey him. And so it was decided to make an appeal for two hundred new workers. In a typically direct and unemotional letter to all the friends and supporters of the Mission, the general director wrote to state the case.

In Australia and New Zealand, in North America and Great Britain, the appeal went forth. Pamphlets and cards were printed and meetings convened to make known the spiritual need of China and the new response that it had called forth from the Mission. Prayer was being made definitely for two hundred new recruits to be on their way to China before the end of 1931. What would be the answer of God?

D. E. Hoste well knew that a big thing was being asked. It meant the sending out of more than twice the average number of new workers for two years. The substantial increase in the Mission's income that would be necessary occasioned no undue concern. "God's work done in God's way will never lack God's supplies" was a principle which applied every bit as much in 1929 as in Hudson Taylor's day. But Hoste knew that such advance into the kingdom of the god of this world would not be uncontested.

"It will involve perhaps the most tremendous conflict which we have yet had as a Mission," he said, "and every part of it will need to be, as it were, steeped in prayer."

The urgent necessity for prayer became apparent as the months passed. Many offers of service came in, yet only one in six proved suitable. Poor health, age, or other difficulties hindered the remainder; for there could be no lowering of the standard of natural and spiritual qualifications in those sent out in order to obtain a numerical objective. By the end of 1930 less than half the required number of new workers had sailed for China – just one more year remained for about one hundred and ten candidates to be accepted, trained, and sent forth if the prayer for two hundred before the end of 1931 was to receive its full answer.

Early in 1931, D. E. Hoste visited England. Sitting in the board room at Newington Green, with W. H. Aldis, the home director, and other members of the London staff, he faced the facts. The figures were presented to him; and he saw how many had already sailed of the number prayed for, how many were in training, and how many were ready to come into training. And as the figures were given, those from Australasia and America as well as from Great Britain, the men sitting around the long table realized they were up against an impossible situation. The Forward Movement had been made widely known in all the home centers. The call for prayer that two hundred new workers should be sent forth before 1931 closed had been publicly made, and with it the firm assurance had been expressed that God would answer!

It was no time for the easy "believism" which accepts defeat and calls it "the will of God." That the name of the Mission would be in disrepute if two hundred qualified workers were not sent out before the year closed mattered little. That doubt would be cast upon the name of the God who answers prayer if they were not forthcoming mattered much. No one in the room that afternoon had any serious doubt that the Forward Movement was the practical outworking of an impelling urge of the Spirit of God. The appeal for the two hundred was no publicity "stunt" to attract attention, but a call for a required number of laborers to fulfil a plan decided upon after much prayer, and with the inward conviction that it was God's will. Yet the answer was being delayed. Somehow there was still conflict in the spiritual realm, and D. E. Hoste was conscious that the powers of darkness had not yet been overcome. There was stillness in the board room as he spoke.

"We must have a day of prayer," he said.

Tuesday, February 10, was set aside to be given up entirely to prayer that God would yet grant their request for the full number of two hundred new workers to be sent out before the end of the year. Cables were sent to North America, Australia, New Zealand and Shanghai, calling as many as possible in the fellowship of the Mission to unite in pleading with God on this day. And God answered! How often in the annals of the

Mission has earnest, united prayer proved effective, and turned into victory what looked like being defeat and confusion of face. From February 10 onwards the tide began to turn. The general director wrote *An Urgent Call to Action,* a leaflet which must have been read by thousands of people. Applications began to come in from promising young people at such a rate that W. H. Aldis announced at the London annual meetings that now there were actually more than the full two hundred candidates in view! And although there were many disappointments and unforeseen hindrances put in the way of the recruits, by the end of the year two hundred and three new workers had set sail for China – the last party, six young men, leaving England on December 31!

Meanwhile, D. E. Hoste had returned to China. He was seventy years old now, and he felt he should retire – yet who was there to take his place? He brought the matter up himself at one council meeting, and it was unanimously decided to ask him to remain in office until further light was given as to who should be his successor. To James Stark, secretary of the Mission, who was, perhaps, his closest friend, he often spoke on the subject. Should he retire now? The question came again and again; and the quiet answer was given that if his time to retire had come, the Lord would reveal who was to take his place. It certainly seemed evident that he must continue for a while. The appointments of G. W. Gibb as a China director and W. H. Warren as assistant China director eased his burden somewhat, but final responsibility still rested upon him.

It was in new and far more commodious surroundings that D. E. Hoste spent his few remaining years as general director. The overruling hand of God was in the removal of Mission headquarters from the old compound in Wusung Road to the spacious building in Sinza Road. For a long time, the Mission home had provided but cramped accommodation for the many missionaries coming from and going to the interior, and for the offices and flats required by headquarters staff. What was later seen to be divine guidance led to the sale of the old premises at such a surprisingly high price that the sum received covered the cost of erecting two great blocks of five-storied buildings on a large piece of ground in another part of Shanghai. From the balcony of his quiet flat, the general director looked down on lawns and tree-shaded walks. Grateful indeed he must have been for such surroundings; but when, a few months later, fighting broke out between the Chinese and Japanese in the very area in which the old premises were situated, a still deeper cause for praise and thanksgiving was seen, for in Sinza Road things remained undisturbed.

The two hundred were arriving in China at a time of seething internal unrest. In the northwest a Moslem rebellion raged. Farther south the Reds were in control of large areas, while brigandage was rife throughout almost the whole land. Added to all this there was famine in North China, bringing famine fever and typhus in its train. The designations of the young workers, inexperienced and with little knowledge of the language, was no light matter. It had been decided that in the allocation of workers to various spheres of service, the unevangelized regions should be given first consideration. Yet the difficulties and dangers which lay in the way of carrying out the carefully planned Forward Movement became increasingly evident. The practical responsibility of those at home was largely fulfilled when the last of the two hundred left the shores of England *en route* for China. For the general director in Shanghai, however, the responsibility increased as the recruits arrived; and as he and the China council faced the various problems confronting them, they realized that for them the Forward Movement was only just beginning.

During the last council meetings held in 1931 they placed on record their "deepened sense of the need of persevering, earnest prayer on the part of the whole Mission and its supporters for the power, guidance, and keeping of the Holy Spirit in carrying it out." Without this there was a danger lest the aim of widespread evangelism be lost sight of, and of the new recruits becoming absorbed in already existing work. But in spite of all the adverse conditions in China, advance was made. 1932 saw eighteen new centers opened. The following year sixteen more were occupied.

In 1934 twelve more were added. From the sending out of the appeal for the two hundred in 1929, over eighty new centers had been opened.

Were there disappointments? Yes. Were there any mistakes made? Were there failures? Yes, there were apparent failures – spiritual defeat when the powers of darkness seemed to swamp the work of God. Let those who have never engaged in spiritual warfare deny its grim reality! Nevertheless, the Forward Movement *was* a forward movement. As D. E. Hoste once quaintly prayed, "Lord, make it a real forward movement; do not let it be a standstill movement, do not let it be a sit-down and go-to-sleep movement!"

The matter of his retirement could not be delayed much longer. Who was God's choice for the future of the Mission? Again and again, in public and private, the matter was discussed. One whom he himself had hoped would be suitable was not acceptable to all. Another declined the position. Meanwhile, his own health was failing; and in 1933 and 1934 he had to go to Chefoo for prolonged rest. It was obvious that he could not continue much longer to carry the burden of responsibility.

Away in England God was preparing one who was to take his place; but that preparation was going on so silently and unobtrusively that none, perhaps, knew of it at the time. When it was at last decided that G. W. Gibb, with his intimate knowledge of the Mission, should be appointed as general director, Frank Houghton, not yet forty years of age, was still detained after his first furlough to assist at London headquarters. Not until the following year did he return to China.

The day came for the council meeting at which Hoste was to announce his retirement. It was in June, 1935, and Shanghai lay in the humid heat of early summer. In the council chamber at Mission headquarters, the general director rose to his feet. The men who sat round the long table were deeply conscious of the solemnity of the occasion. For thirty-five years he had taken his place as chairman of the China council. For thirty-five years the responsibility for decisions made had rested with him. For thirty-five years he had consistently sacrificed his own interests and desires for the Mission of which God had made him the leader.

Steadily through those years the work had progressed. There were 1,360 missionaries where there had been 780. From 364 organized churches the number had grown to over 1,200. 400 outstations were reported in 1903, and over 2,200 in 1935. The number of baptisms each year had increased from 1,700 to 7,500. And now the man who had been at the center of it all, praying, planning, guiding, spoke to those who had been his fellow laborers through the years.

His manner, usually so cautious, was surprisingly bright and optimistic. Turning to G. W. Gibb, who was to take his place, he assured him that the Lord would do more than all he could ask or think. He would never fail. God was infinitely rich in resources, and personally he rejoiced in the knowledge that every need would be abundantly met, if not through one channel, then through another. The work, he asserted, was the Lord's. He would amply care for it and for the workers.

He spoke with unusual spontaneity. The members of the China council, whose hearts had been somewhat weighed down with difficult Mission problems, looked almost with surprise at the one whom they had known for so long. He seemed eased, as one who has laid down at last a heavy burden, or carried through some vital business committed to him.

He referred to matters of finance, and the relationship of the home centers to the work on the field. Then, as he looked round the table, speaking for the last time as the general director of the Mission, the source of the strength that had sustained him through the years, when the pressure of responsibility had sometimes seemed almost unbearable, was revealed. "Count on God!" he said, and there was the confidence born of long experience in his voice. "Count on God for the future. Reckon on his faithfulness!"

Chapter Twelve

That Which Remained

JAPANESE mechanized units sped noisily through the smooth, tree-shaded roads of the international settlement in Shanghai.

Outside the main gates of the China Inland Mission compound Japanese guards took up their position. The land of the Rising Sun was at open war with the U.S.A. and Great Britain. It was over six years since D. E. Hoste and his wife had retired to the little three-roomed flat on the second floor of the Mission home. Pleasant years they had been for him. He was still at the headquarters of the Mission, meeting with those who came and went on the busy compound. Almost daily he saw the men who had been his colleagues, and on whom the leadership of the work now devolved. The burden of responsibility was his no more, but his life had been too closely entwined in the Mission's life for him to be happy separated from it. And at last he was free to enjoy the comfort of home and the companionship of his wife. "We spend a good deal more time together now than used to be possible," he wrote, "and so our lives tend to unite, as it were, in one channel – a great gain to me, I can truly say."

One of his sons lived in Shanghai, and his wife and children visited the Mission compound often. Hoste had always longed for a daughter, and now his well-known affection for little girls found its outlet in the companionship of his own granddaughters. And how he delighted in discussions on world affairs with the son whom he had had so little opportunity of seeing during the strenuous years of his directorship!

The strain of those years had told on him, however; and although physically his health improved, his memory began to fail. Names by the hundred he had been able to remember, but now he found them eluding him, and his prayers became more general. It was strange to him to see a face which was familiar and yet to have to admit he had forgotten the name of the person he was addressing.

"It's my memory," he would explain in courteous apology.

When he retired, his life work finished, he thought he would not live much longer.

"During the past year or so the solemn truth – for it is such – that I shall have before long to appear before the judgment seat of Christ ... has been much in my mind," he wrote in 1935. Yet now, in December, 1941, as he looked out on the Japanese soldiers who were taking possession of the neighboring compound, he was well, and still comparatively active.

After the first tense uncertainty of wondering how the Japanese would act towards the hundreds of "enemy nationals" living in Shanghai had passed, life continued comparatively normally on the big Mission compound. Certain restrictions were imposed, but for months the missionaries were allowed to remain in their own homes instead of being swept off to internment camps as had seemed probable. But internment came at last. First one group, then another, left the Mission compound, carrying bags and bundles as they passed, "like them that go into captivity," out through the big gates. And as each group departed, two figures stood to bid them farewell. Slim and erect, D. E. Hoste, with his wife, watched them go, waving goodbye to the members of their Mission family whom they would probably never see again.

The time came, however, when they, too, had to leave. The Japanese had issued certificates of "temporary exemption" to the aged and sick people – but the China Inland Mission premises must be vacated, and those who had remained there were housed in a nearby missionary home in Tifang Road. And so, one April day, the white-haired, soldierly figure descended the wide stairs for the last time, and with his wife stepped into a double rickshaw. A group of Chinese had gathered to see the last contingent leave; and as the aged couple, composed and smiling, passed along the wide path that ran between a fresh green lawn and shrubs where waxy-white magnolias gleamed, someone murmured tearfully: "We shall never see them again. They'll never come back!" And they never did.

The missionary home to which they, together with thirteen others, were sent, usually accommodated about twenty to twenty-five people. Now forty had to be fitted in somehow – and only three of them were under sixty years of age! The quiet privacy to which D. E. Hoste had been accustomed for so many years was his no more. There was little opportunity for solitude in the crowded house. Mrs. Hoste was ill; and he must share the room, not only with her, but also with the one who nursed her. At eighty the mind that had grappled for years with many and complex matters was unable to readjust itself to the new situation. He was living under strain once more – and for him strain had long been associated with the direction of the Mission and its affairs. Every now and again he would fancy himself back in the council chamber. He must concentrate! He must lead some matter through to a right conclusion! The weary mind was trying to grasp something that eluded it; and while the presence of a nurse in the room did not appear to strike him as incongruous, it disturbed him subconsciously. Gravely and courteously, he would ask her to withdraw, as there was a council meeting in progress! Then, as she slipped quietly on to the little veranda, understanding something of the reactions of the over-tired brain, he would settle down again and relax. When she returned he would be normal once more – patiently accepting the strange situation which he could not completely understand.

He loved to pray. Always he had a world vision, though naturally China claimed a larger share of his intercessions than any other country. For years the scriptural injunction to make supplications for all men, for kings, and all that are in authority had been faithfully observed; and realizing Russia's increasing political power, he prayed earnestly for "Mr. Stalin and his colleagues." Perhaps his greatest burden, however, was for a spiritual revival in England, such as he had known in his youth. Oh, for such men as Wesley or Moody, to turn multitudes to God! Often he enquired if there was any news of such a one, and seemed surprised when the answer was always in the negative.

It was exactly a year after their arrival at the missionary home that his wife died. For months she had been ill, and it was evident that she could not recover. The gentle, fragrant life, for so long lived in quiet seclusion as a semi-invalid, was ebbing away; and as he sat beside her bed, hour after hour, watching her go, the tears rolled slowly and unrestrainedly down his cheeks. For fifty years she had been his companion and the greatest comfort of his life. He could always depend on her sympathy and understanding. Yet in spite of her physical weakness she had never made claims on his time and attention. The work of God committed to him must always come before more natural claims. And now she was going.... On April 12 she died.

The funeral was held in the Bubbling Well Church. What would the ceremony be like, those from the missionary home wondered? Fellow missionaries were interned; D. E. Hoste's son was in a military camp, and his daughter-in-law and grandchildren were confined elsewhere. Some of the German missionaries who were in Shanghai would come, no doubt – their faithfulness and loving sympathy had never failed. But the Chinese, the people for whom a lifetime of service had been given, could scarcely be expected to attend the funeral of an "enemy national" and risk arousing the suspicions of the Japanese!

Up the straight, flagged path of the cemetery and into the church walked D. E. Hoste, immaculate and dignified. The scent from masses of flowers pervaded the building; and as the old man entered, those who accompanied him saw with surprise that the place was crowded with people! German missionaries formed a choir. Officials were there from the Swiss consulate, out of respect for one who had been a well-known figure in Shanghai for forty years. Chinese Christians and church leaders, rows of them, stood as the white-haired, erect figure walked alone up the aisle to the front of the church, where his daughter-in-law and grandchildren, brought by a sympathetic Japanese official from their place of internment, awaited him! And after the solemnly triumphant service had started, another figure walked up the aisle to take his place between his father and wife – D. E. Hoste's second son, who had been permitted to come, under escort, from the military camp where he was interned, to attend his mother's funeral.

Little opportunity was given for father and son to speak. Perhaps they did not need to say much. One word was sufficient to nerve them anew for what lay ahead as they parted once more by the graveside. The family motto of the Hostes had come to have a new meaning for them both, with its word that had inspired their ancestors before them: *"Fortitudine!"*

Two months later the inmates of the missionary home had to move again – this time to an internment camp. The temporary exemption granted to aged and sick people was canceled; and on June 28, 1944, more than three hundred of them had to assemble at the Columbia Country Club. Through the streets of Shanghai they went – some in ambulances, some on stretchers, some on beds, some walking slowly, supporting those weaker than themselves, or leading the blind. Amongst them was D. E. Hoste, slightly confused, not understanding the situation, but patiently accepting it.

The old people were taken to a compound in which were eight residences, formerly occupied by the staff of the Bank of China and requisitioned by Japanese military units when they occupied the international settlement. Many were the prayers that went up from the hearts of the small group of China Inland Mission members for the man who had been for so long their leader. Very dependent on them he was now, and they longed to ease things for him. They rejoiced greatly when he was permitted a tiny, cell-like room to himself, for the crowds worried him, bringing a sense of strain which he did not understand and could not always hide.

He was growing weaker, and spent much time on his bed, gazing contentedly out of the little window of his room. He could see the boughs of a tree, and seemed to derive unfailing delight from just looking at it. It spoke to him of the beauty of his heavenly Father's creation.

He never complained, however bad the camp food was; but when some dainty was provided by those who often sacrificed their own small stores that he might have something appetizing, he noticed it immediately and ate it first! He did not know where it came from, but was unfailingly grateful for every kindness shown him. In the camp, where there was often a good deal of looseness of conversation and manner, he was always courteous, scrupulously tidy, and he retained a quiet dignity which impressed those who met him.

The joy and refreshment of his life was prayer. How his face would light up when someone came to his room and said, "Would you like to pray, Mr. Hoste?" As always, the presence of another helped; and he would pray freely, pouring out his heart to God, pleading again and again for such men as Wesley and Moody to be raised up, or interceding for Chinese church leaders. In the midst of the restlessness of camp, the little room where he lay was like a sanctuary; and those who visited him were conscious of another Presence there.

Although Japan surrendered in August, 1945, it was not until October that final relief from the internment camp came. But at last the day arrived when D. E. Hoste was carried on board the *Oxfordshire*, with one of the doctors of his own Mission to attend him as he sailed back to England for the last time.

· · · · ·

"When thou wast young, thou girdest thyself, and walkest whither thou wouldest; but when thou shalt be old, thou shalt stretch forth thy hands, and another shall gird thee, and carry thee whither thou wouldest not. This spake he, signifying by what death he should glorify God."

The old man lay in a quiet little bedroom in the Mildmay Nursing Home. He was ill and very tired, and seemed content to lie still most of the time, gazing out of the window. Old colleagues visited him; and he greeted them with quiet formality, obviously at a complete loss as to their identity. While they were there he tried to talk. Fragments of sentences, such as he must often have used in council meetings, were painstakingly framed. "In my opinion, his unsuitability lies in the attitude … The logical sequence of the matter would be.…" But often he seemed completely detached from the country to which he had given his life, and the Mission in which he had served her. He looked calmly uninterested when China was mentioned, and the announcement that a visitor was a missionary of the China Inland Mission left him unmoved. Disconnected reminiscences of his schooldays and occasional references to the Cambridge Seven came more readily than any memories of later years. But the faculty of memory was really worn out, and the well-disciplined mind was too tired to grasp things. Even prayer, to which he was so well accustomed, seemed an effort.

One day two visitors went to see him. With his usual studied politeness he endeavored to converse with them and answer their questions.

"Do you like flowers?" one visitor asked, noticing that there were none in the room.

"Yes," he answered indifferently. He paused for a moment. Flowers. "Not particularly." What were the impressions that the thought of flowers made on this man who had burnt himself out in the life to which he had been called? Fragrant, beautiful, speaking of the softer things of life, flowers have little part in the life of a soldier. Even their graves are often bereft of them.

"I'm thankful I never settled down into family life," he continued slowly. "Thankful.…"

His visitors were silent. He was speaking more to himself than to them. The rival claims of his family and the demands of the work of which he was the leader must often have come before him. He had sometimes seemed almost ruthless in his devotion to what he deemed his first duty. How deep must the knife pierce? "If any man hates not his father and mother, son and daughter, yea, and his own life also, he cannot be my disciple."

Life lay behind him now – its joys and sorrows, its disappointments and triumphs were over. Very soon he would have to give account of himself to God; with calm eyes, he looked beyond his visitors and lapsed into silence, but the words he had just spoken seemed to linger. There was stillness for a minute or two.

Then they spoke again. Fragments of sentences came from him occasionally, but he was obviously finding it hard to understand the situation. Something was eluding him. But suddenly he seemed transported.

"The Beatific Vision," he said, gazing out of the window by his bed, his eyes strangely alight. He seemed to be looking at that which to them was yet unseen. They listened eagerly to hear – what was the beatific vision?

"I could weep when I think of Jesus," he said, his voice lingering over the beloved name. "To see Jesus – that is the Beatific Vision."

• • • • •

On May 11, 1946, as the sun was rising over London, God called his soldier home.

Extracts from Letters

"When God raises up a man for special service, he first works in that man the principles which later on are, through his labors and influence, to be the means of widespread blessing to the church and the world." So wrote D. E. Hoste in the Introduction to the biography of his leader and hero, Hudson Taylor. What applied in the life of the founder of the China Inland Mission applied also in the life of the one who later became its leader. God worked in him the principles of that true humility which willingly accepts the lower place and does not strive; the sustained discipline which never relaxes in its vigil against the subtle temptation to self-indulgence; the leadership which works by co-operation and example, rather than the ruthless exercise of authority. He learned deep secrets as he went on doing the will of his Master, and some of those secrets were divulged in the letters and articles he wrote for the benefit of fellow missionaries of whom he had been entrusted with the oversight. From these writings, and a few of his addresses, have been culled D. E. Hoste's comments on some of the vital principles governing our relationship to God and our fellow men.

A clear thinker, with vision and sound judgment, he could express himself in a way that left no doubt as to his meaning in the minds of those he addressed. Few flashes of genius came from his pen, but rather steadily-gleaming gems of simply expressed spiritual truth, words that had been tried in the fires of personal experience. Because the gifts of leadership and colleagueship, the qualities of zeal and humility, the exercise of prayer and self-discipline were so apparent in his own life, what he has to say on these subjects carries conviction.

"If I have any gift at all," he said once, "I feel it is along the lines of applying Christian principles to life."

Spiritual Leadership

WHAT is the essential difference between spurious and true Christian leadership? When a man, in virtue of an official position in the church, demands the obedience of another, irrespective of the latter's reason and conscience, this is the spirit of tyranny. When, on the other hand, by the exercise of tact and sympathy, by prayer, spiritual power and sound wisdom, one Christian worker is able to influence and enlighten another, so that the latter, through the medium of his own reason and conscience, is led to alter one course and adopt another, this is true spiritual leadership.

• • • • •

The faculty of keeping an open mind until all the facts and circumstances bearing upon a question have been ascertained is by no means common; and yet for the right guidance and management of complex affairs, it is obviously essential. I have had occasion repeatedly to observe that individuals gifted in some respects are sadly lacking in the quality mentioned; and yet unless the one in a central position is careful to hear and weigh all that has to be said touching the different aspects of a given affair, he will not be in a position either to reach a sound conclusion or to carry with him the consent and confidence of those affected by that conclusion. In affairs there is a good deal that passes for strength which is essentially weakness.

• • • • •

I venture to think that the essence of a general director's ministry, instead of wanting to do things directly himself, is to help as required and to influence others. Direct action of one's own is far easier than work accomplished through others. They are indeed two entirely different forms of ministry. Hence the practical difficulty and even danger connected with the efforts of a man accustomed to doing things himself rather than contributing, as asked, to the action of another. So far as my experience goes, there are few things calling for more deep and consistent self-discipline and self-humbling than the realization of this ideal.

* * * * *

Perhaps the most important, and in some ways the most difficult part of a general director's functions lies in the exercise of helpful influence on the minds and so on the work of important colleagues. For such a purpose he needs indeed to "speak as the oracles of God," which, as I think we shall agree, involves a holy fear and trembling as to his own state of heart before God and in relation to his brethren. Unless he is constantly and faithfully wrestling in the heavenlies with the powers of darkness, there is real danger of his becoming involved in wrestling with his colleagues. As the Scripture says, "The servant of the Lord must not strive, but be gentle." In this connection I have myself often been reminded of our Lord's teaching that it will not be easy to obtain the bread wherewith to feed others. "How forcible are right words!" And again, "The word in season, how good it is!" But such words are not easy to obtain.

Qualification for Leadership.

My personal judgment, for what it may be worth, is that capacity to appreciate the gifts and powers of widely varying kinds of workers, and then to help them along the lines of their own personalities and working, is the main quality for oversight in a mission like ours.

Experience has confirmed to me the great importance of thorough and comprehensive knowledge of a man, obtained by observing him in different spheres and relationships. In some respects ——— was undoubtedly fitted; but as time went on, and one had increasing opportunities of really gauging his mental caliber, the more I was obliged to recognize that he did not possess the amplitude of mind necessary for appreciating and learning from the thought and experience of others, and then weaving it into his own thinking and arrangements. History shows that this faculty has, as a rule, been possessed by great political and military leaders. Napoleon, for instance (perhaps the greatest of them all), had a council composed of able men, each with special knowledge and experience in some one line of public matters, such as foreign affairs, finance, police, making of roads and other departments of civil engineering bearing upon communication, sanitation, etc. He was a good listener and possessed in a high degree the gift of applying the special knowledge of others to a particular set of circumstances. Doesn't history show that every truly great man is more or less made on these lines?

・・・・・

It is the old and fundamental question of the measure of a man's humility and his capacity, as far as circumstances admit, to hear and profit by a wide range of opinion. It was the apostle Paul who in a transcendent measure was granted a unique revelation and ministry, who also enforced the principle contained in the words, "By that which every joint supplieth." This requires self-discipline in willingness to wait before reaching a conclusion such as is not very common. It may sound a paradox, but I venture to believe it right that the habit of taking it for granted that one is able to set other people to rights without taking the time and trouble to acquaint oneself fully with their views and the reasons for them is a pretty sure mark of unfitness for the highest kind of leadership.

Conditions of True Success

As time goes on, I become increasingly persuaded that the spiritual and moral qualities requisite for helpful dealing with church affairs and guiding other workers are to be found quite as much in men and women drawn from one social stratum as from another. The practical point is that they are really men and women of prayer, deeply distrustful of their own judgment and impulses, only forming opinions and expressing them as taught and guided by the Holy Spirit. We come back to the holy but fundamental truth that it is the spiritual that is the practical.

* * * * *

It is sadly possible, unless we carefully maintain the habit of spending a long time daily in intercession and prayer, also in study and meditation upon the Holy Scriptures and upon the books of godly teachers thereon, instead of going on from strength to strength and experiencing increasing gift and power, to undergo a subtle but deeply real process of deterioration. In this matter more perhaps than anything else, it remains true that "God is not mocked." If we are faithful and diligent daily in thus giving ourselves to prayer, earnest study of Scripture and meditation thereon, with a view not only to our personal edification such as every believer needs, but in order that we may be equipped for our service of preaching and teaching others, then we may humbly expect to grow in usefulness and power as preachers and Bible teachers, as well as fellow-helpers with and wise, sympathetic counselors of our Chinese colleagues. Experience more and more demonstrates the un-wisdom of predictions as to leadership in the work of one or another. It is well to recognize that this mainly depends upon the faithful, persevering fulfillment of the laws of progress.

* * * * *

In a mission like ours, those guiding its affairs must be prepared to put up with waywardness and opposition and be able to desist from courses of action which, though they may be intrinsically sound and beneficial, are not approved by some of those affected. I shall never forget the impression made upon me by Mr. Taylor in connection with these affairs. Again and again, he was obliged either greatly to modify or lay aside projects which are sound and helpful, but met with determined opposition, and so tended to create greater evils than those which might have been removed or mitigated by the changes in question. Later on, in answer to patient continuance in prayer, many of such projects were given effect to. Patient, persevering prayer plays a more vital and practical part in the development of the Mission's work than most people have any idea of.

Preparation for Leadership

In connection with the call of Gideon the question naturally arises, in what sense and for what reason was he designated by the Lord as a mighty man of valor? That there may be room for difference of opinion on this point is true. We venture to think that most probably the fact upon which it was based lay in the steady courage which, by the grace of God, enabled him to continue faithful to Jehovah at a time when the worship of Baal was practiced by his own father and family and also the rest of the inhabitants of his native town. Those who in early life have had to face a situation of this kind, involving a refusal to conform to practices and standards prevailing in the community of which they are a member, know how hard it is faithfully to take and to adhere to such a course. Scripture gives other instances of men subsequently greatly used of God, who in the beginning were severely tested in fidelity to duty in the face of danger or opposition. Sometimes the issue involved may have seemed relatively small and unimportant in itself. David, for example, might easily have argued that the loss of one sheep did not matter much. Hence the part of wisdom was to let the lion go off with his victim. Had he reasoned and acted in this way, it is hard to believe that he would later have been God's anointed king over Israel. Nor would Daniel have become ruler of a great empire had he compromised in the initial test of the food he was to eat. The words of our Lord are vitally true. "He that is faithful in that which is least is faithful also in much."

⋅ ⋅ ⋅ ⋅ ⋅

Are our loved ones taken from us, our health and strength reduced, or our pecuniary resources diminished? Is our outward sphere of service curtailed, is our good name attacked? In each and in all of these circumstances we may with confidence remember that God is providing "some better thing" for us, and that in no other way can we be led on into this higher and richer experience. Those who are appointed to exercise spiritual oversight must needs be prepared for their ministry in this way.

⋅ ⋅ ⋅ ⋅ ⋅

Painful as it was, the prolonged discipline of suffering and danger through which David had to pass was necessary if he was to be preserved from failure similar to that of Saul, when in his turn subjected to the trials and temptations of the kingly office. Let not those, therefore, who are desirous of being fruitful in God's work be unduly cast down if for a portion, at any rate, of their lives they find their plans are thwarted, and they themselves discredited and humiliated. Then is the time to act upon the injunction to "humble ourselves under the mighty hand of God," and to learn to be as a weaned child before him, and thus to be purged from that self-will and self-energy which are prone to operate with subtle but deadly effect in undisciplined lives.

⋅ ⋅ ⋅ ⋅ ⋅

Should any feel their present sphere to be either too narrow or too uncongenial, it is well to bear in mind that by failing to "let patience have its perfect work," and insisting upon being given a position more in consonance with what they think to be due to them, they may render it morally impossible for the God of Abraham to fit them for the service which he desires to accomplish through them later on.

Towards Unity

It is probably true to say that every servant of the Lord desires to be an instrument of blessing in his hand. The fulfillment of this desire may often depend upon the union of two hitherto divided and mutually antagonistic individuals or communities. The long period of mutual enmity between Judah and Israel was, we learn from Scripture, marked by wars which deepened the estrangement and rendered the restoration of unity all the more difficult. The same, alas, may sometimes be true now. We do well to ask ourselves whether one reason for lack of greater progress and fruitfulness in our work may not be due to a lack of adjustment with some other servant or servants of the Lord. Are we prepared to take steps essential to healing such division? We are commanded to lay aside ill-will, confessing our faults one to another and humbling ourselves in order that such breaches may be healed.

• • • • •

The duty of, as far as possible, putting right any wrong done to another, is given an early and prominent place in our Lord's teaching of his disciples, as recorded in Matt. 5:23-24: "If thou bring thy gift to the altar and there rememberest that thy brother hath ought against thee, leave there thy gift before the altar and go thy way: first be reconciled to thy brother, and then come and offer thy gift." That is to say, the acceptance of ourselves and our gifts by the Lord is vitally affected by our relations with our fellows. It is to be feared that not infrequently barrenness both in personal experience and in service may be due to some disregard of this precept.

I sometimes feel that we Evangelicals are perhaps specially in danger of losing sight of this aspect of truth and so without realizing it, becoming hardened by the deceitfulness of sin and being out of real communion with the Lord.

• • • • •

Sin of any kind grieves the Holy Spirit, but that form of it which finds expression in bitterness towards another child of God causes him special pain; just as, conversely, love and unity amongst the Lord's people draws forth in a special degree his favor and blessing. Should not the remembrance of the wonderful patience exercised toward us by our divine Comforter cause us to be patient toward one another? If the Holy Spirit, in spite of so much in us and our ways to grieve him, does not leave us, we should be very slow to conclude that we cannot work with some other Christian. The sense of our own ignorance and proneness to err may well work in us a spirit of gentleness and forbearance toward our fellow believers, whose previous advantages and opportunities may have been less than our own.

It might have been expected that the Lord, at whose command Abraham had left his native land and its cherished associations, would see to it that his companion should be thoroughly congenial and helpful. But it was not so. On the contrary, it is clear that, whilst Lot seems to have had a measure of faith, he was weak, selfish, and unspiritual, and therefore a cause of strain and anxiety rather than of strength and comfort. And yet we may be sure that the trial and discipline this involved were necessary to the forming of Abraham's character and of working in him the moral and spiritual qualities essential to his being a "father of many nations." It was not a matter of a course of special study of the history and characteristics of the races and countries then upon the earth. His fitness for the future depended rather upon his maintaining the right attitude toward one individual, Lot. The discipline involved was searching and the temptation no doubt was strong to lose patience and either become negatively cold and critical towards him or summarily to terminate the connection. The magnanimous, yielding spirit evinced by Abraham when the separation became inevitable shows his attainment through trial of a right spirit such as fitted him for far-reaching usefulness. Further, when Lot and his family were carried off by the hostile kings, Abraham did not, as he might have done, leave him to reap the results of his own sin and mistakes. At the risk of danger and loss to himself and his own household he rescued his brother.

The Oracles of God

It is a fact that our minds cannot receive correct impressions of God's plan and methods for the carrying on of the work unless much time is given to waiting upon him. Nor will there be spiritual power in our public ministry for the conversion of souls and the real feeding of the flock of God without prolonged and strenuous supplications.

* * * * *

I remember being early impressed by our Lord's teaching that it would not be easy to obtain the right words, whether for a number or for an individual, whether Christian or pagan. "I tell you," he said, "he will not give him because he is his friend (ye are my friends if ye do whatsoever I command you), but because he wearied him." How much do we know of prevailing importunity for bread with which to feed others? He is no respecter of persons; it is the one who recognizes the true nature of his vocation as a worker for Christ and gives himself to importunate prayer for bread with which to feed others, whether fellow workers, church members, or unbelievers, who will be useful. How often have I for days waited in earnest prayer for right words in replying to a letter dealing with some trouble or difficulty in a district or station. "If any man speaks, let him speak as the oracles of God." "It is not in me; God shall give Pharaoh an answer of peace," said Joseph of old. That was not a pose or polite phrase, but a simple, fundamental fact.

* * * * *

It is only in so far as through actual experience I am led into the power of the kingdom that I can be used truly to help and lead my brethren into a deeper knowledge of Christ and his fellowship. I find the need of daily spending much time in secret communion with the Lord if my senses are to be exercised either to discern the state of my brethren or to minister the word in season to them.

I cannot afford to take up an independent attitude of mind toward any of my brethren, whether young or old; nor can I rely upon past experiences as my present relationship with him. It is by earnest, persevering waiting upon him in secret that my senses are exercised to perceive and to transmit his message. The imparting of head knowledge, however true and valuable, as a means, tends to blind and hinder in so far as it becomes regarded as an end in itself. Is the need of waiting upon God for messages given a sufficient place in our teaching of others? How true it is that the Lord is no respecter of persons. I expect we have both often had the experience of receiving spiritual help and refreshment through some quite young brother or sister who is experimentally joined to the Lord, whilst there has been a sad lack of such refreshment in intercourse with some of much greater maturity.

It is morally impossible to exercise trust in God while there is failure to wait upon him for guidance and direction. The man who does not learn to wait upon the Lord and have his thoughts molded by him will never possess that steady purpose and calm trust which is essential to the exercise of wise influence upon others in times of crisis and difficulty.

The One Thing Needful

A source of spiritual weakness and defeat may be found in failure jealously to guard our time of secret prayer and study of God's Word. These are needed not only for our own soul's nourishment, but as part of our work and ministry on behalf of others. It is easy by negligence in these things to grieve and partially quench the Holy Spirit, the consequence being that without our knowing it, we are living and working on a lower plane of blessing and efficiency than we otherwise might do. A practical way of testing ourselves in this matter is to apply the question: are we spending as much time in prayer and feeding upon God's Word as we do in taking bodily nourishment at meals? It is those who habitually draw nigh to God, who will find that he draws nigh to them and uses them as his messengers to others.

• • • • •

I find it a good thing to fast. I do not lay down rules for anyone in this matter, but I know it has been a good thing for me to go without meals to get time for prayer. So many say they have not sufficient time to pray. We think nothing of spending an hour or two in taking our meals. It is worthwhile trying out doing without sometimes. What a benefit it is spiritually, and I believe our digestions would benefit also!

• • • • •

Shall we not do well to take to heart afresh the great fact that, after all, the interests and issues involved in the preaching of the gospel amongst men are both more far-reaching and permanent in their importance than anything else can be? If our vision of the unseen and eternal is to be kept bright and true, how important it is that we be found faithful in our daily personal communion with the Lord himself through earnest prayer and study of his holy Word.

Thus, and thus only, shall we be preserved, whether from the temptations and snares of the devil and allurements of the world, or in the hour of depression and sorrow.

• • • • •

If one may speak for others, the danger of spiritual stagnation or even retrogression is one that needs to be constantly guarded against. Our numbers are so few, and the calls upon our time and strength are often so heavy, that the taking of time for, by prayer and study, maintaining and enriching our own spiritual lives, and our power to influence others aright, becomes exceedingly difficult; and yet this is the one thing needful.

In connection with the training home, the thought sometimes comes to me, in view of the growing emphasis on prayer and intercession in those parts of the field where there has been special spiritual blessing, whether the exercise of them should not have a more definite and larger place in the course of preparation. The leadership would need to be by someone who, through much exercise and even travail, has himself been baptized with a true and fervent spirit of prayer.

Should it not be recognized that the practice of prayer and intercession needs to be taught to young believers, or rather developed in young believers, quite as much, if not more so than other branches of the curriculum? Unless, however, we ourselves are, through constant, persevering practice, truly alive unto God in this holy warfare, we shall be ineffective in influencing others. I am quite sure the rule holds that the more we pray the more we want to pray; the converse also being true.

True Humility

The record of the circumstances connected with our Lord's birth and early youth illustrates certain important principles relating to the spread of God's kingdom upon earth. It might have been thought that every advantage which worldly position and wealth could give would have been provided by God for his Son in entering upon his life and ministry. It was far otherwise. From the beginning to the end of his life, our Lord was entirely without the aid which influence of the kind referred to might be supposed to give him and the cause which he had at heart. He came into the world as one of a despised and conquered race, and, moreover, as a member of the poor and humble class in his own nation.

We see how Herod succeeded for a time in driving him out of Judaea, and it is instructive to notice that God did not intervene by the exercise of any special power to prevent the Lord Jesus being driven down into Egypt.... The whole train of events is a living commentary upon our Lord's own words, "Resist not evil." And we are reminded afresh of the great truth that it is in simple, unreserved obedience to these principles that the work of God, whether in an individual or as a whole, will grow and permanently prosper. The life that is thus governed must expect to suffer loss and to be kept out of seeming advantages.

• • • • •

"Showing all meekness unto all men." The very word "meekness" implies that there has been wrong treatment, calling, in the Christian, for the exercise of patience, humility, and tenderness of heart and of manner. "He that is hasty of spirit exalteth folly." We do well to remember that failure in this respect goes far to vitiate and render fruitless a ministry which may otherwise be characterized with much real earnestness and ability.

• • • • •

It may safely be said that nothing will more effectively destroy a worker's influence (in China) than a hasty spirit and exhibition of anger.

• • • • •

A jealous watchfulness against injuries, and promptness in making reprisals are, in the estimation of the world, the characteristics of a man of strength and wisdom. In the eyes of the Lord it is, however, far otherwise. He has revealed to us that one of his own attributes is that he is slow to anger.

A calm and patient spirit in the presence of wrong and injustice should be cultivated by every Christian man; but it is especially needful in the case of those entrusted with the high honor of preaching the gospel or exercising oversight amongst the Lord's people. "The beginning of strife is like the letting out of water." It is of vital importance, therefore, if at any time we find ourselves tempted to enter into contention, that we should seek for grace to be kept from doing so, and give ourselves to quiet waiting upon the Lord for his power and guidance. In no other way can we be fitted to deal with the faults and disputes of others without ourselves becoming infected with the spirit of strife and partisanship.

As we see the sins, vices, and follies of others, the tendency for a spirit of bitterness, impatience, and contempt in some degree to possess us is at once strong and subtle. We witness acts of depravity which we ourselves have not committed and are apt to conclude that we are therefore better than persons so behaving. It is the mistake of the Pharisee, who, no doubt sincerely, thanked God that he was not as others; but who our Lord has told us, was nevertheless condemned. He did not perceive that the true measure of guilt of each individual is to be gauged not so much by the character of certain actions, as by the extent to which he has come short of the standard of conduct which God expects of him, having regard to the light and opportunity granted to him. A heartfelt perception of this fundamental truth will help us in forming a true estimate of ourselves as compared with others, and will work in us that spirit of meekness and respect in our contact with our fellow men, without which our efforts for their good are in danger of being fruitless.

· · · · ·

Let us not be dismayed by manifold trials, whether in the form of inward temptations or of outward difficulties and sorrows. These things are inseparable from our service, and, moreover, form an important part of our training as spiritual helpers to others. Meekness and gentleness with those who are out of the way are wrought in us by the knowledge of our own weakness.

"He Humbled Himself"

THINK of Jesus Christ. He was equal with God. That was his right place, at God's right hand. But he chose to forego his rights. He could not have been accused of pride by remaining equal with

God, yet he voluntarily took a lowly place. He gladly chose it. He made himself of no reputation. There was no mere outward semblance of humility covering wrong motive and hidden pride. We are to have this mind, and should be prepared to go down.

· · · · ·

The Son of God became man. Whilst on earth he had every right to the obedience of man, whether as creator, or as the heir to the throne of David, or in virtue of his personal character and conduct. Each and all of these rights were not only ignored but were trampled underfoot, our Lord deliberately refusing to assert or vindicate them by any appeal to power, divine or human. The result was his death and, so far as man was concerned, the defeat of his cause.... May we have grace so to follow in the footsteps of our Lord that our witness as ministers of the gospel may not be impaired, and we may thus be able to approve ourselves as the servants of God. Herein will lie our true victory and fruitfulness; the other method of self-assertion or demanding rights, resulting with equal certainty in spiritual defeat and barrenness.

· · · · ·

We are all familiar with the sad incident of the presumption of Uzzah, and the judgment which overtook him, as the result of which we read that "David was displeased," and, abandoning his purpose of publicly honoring Jehovah, allowed the ark to be carried aside into an obscure home. It amounted to a virtual rejection of the Lord's rightful claim to the central and paramount place; and it is in these circumstances that we read the words, "the Lord blessed Obed-Edom and all his household." How they speak to us of the divine patience and meekness, and of the love that never faileth, and how they stand out in contrast with the littleness and petulance of human nature. Man, when deprived, or kept out of his rightful position, or what he considers to be such, is too ready to give way to bitterness and resentment; and those whose lot is thrown with him in the place of neglect or obscurity too frequently find his presence anything but a comfort and blessing.

May the Lord's servants have grace to follow in the footsteps of their Master, who, in all his dealings with us, perfectly manifested the mind and heart of God. "He came unto his own, and his own received him not." He, the appointed heir to the throne of Israel, was cast out of the inheritance and nailed to a cross, and there we find him bestowing forgiveness and life upon the poor thief who hung at his side, and with his expiring breath invoking blessing on the heads of his enemies. Herein lay his victory over the world at the very time when, to all appearances, the world was triumphing over him.

How easy it is in some measure to lose sight of the fact that the only Christian life is the Christ-life worked out in relation to the circumstances of our lives.

The Secret of Submission

I truly feel for you in the loss of ———, the more so as knowing by experience the value of a God-given friend and colleague; also the corresponding deprivation of strength and comfort due to his removal. That, however, is not so hard to bear as another kind of experience – namely, having a former friend turn against and attack one. As the poet says, "That was the unkindest cut of all." It is not only the stab, but the hand that holds the dagger. As the years have gone by, it has more and more been impressed upon me that one needs to *love God* in such experiences, which I suppose means that we are governed by and act in accordance with his Word and his mind at such times. In that case, the things that are hardest to bear *work together for* our *good*. If, on the other hand, we yield to the temptation to hit back and to strive, then the very things that are intended by the Lord to deepen, sweeten, and enrich our characters will certainly have the opposite effect.

It is only as we are governed by his teaching and his principles that we in any true sense *love God*.

• • • • •

How important it is, when some "brook" (natural comfort, friendship, prosperity, health) in our lives is drying up, not to murmur, or if it is brought about by the misdoings of fellowmen not to let our minds dwell over much on it, lest we become full of bitterness; in which case these things will not work for our good but will work harm. We are told in Romans 8 that "all things work together for good to them that love God." Not to those that God loves, for he loves all. It is necessary to love God practically, in the experience, to maintain a right attitude towards him of quiet confidence in him and faithfulness to him. When your "brook" is drying up – that is the time to love. Then all things will work together for good, and truly the words of the prophet will be fulfilled in our lives that for iron there shall be silver and for brass there shall be gold. God never takes away without wanting to give something better. He takes brass away to give gold – not necessarily earthly but heavenly.

We think of Joseph. All that goes for happiness and satisfaction seems to have been taken out of his life. His elder brothers sold him into Egypt; he begins to prosper, and his reputation is ruined by a wicked woman. Surely the "brook" of his life dried up. But we are told that God was with him and God was doing it. Joseph recognized that, and he said to his brethren, "It was not you, but God." He did not look at the immediate agencies at work. He looked up to God and accepted these things as from him.

• • • • •

To take the lowly place in a misunderstanding; when slighted or hurt to go under the slight or hurt, humbling oneself under the mighty hand of God, relying on him in due season to exalt one, is faith in operation.

Self-discipline

THE danger lest domestic claims should unduly intervene with a missionary's work should be pointed out. The tendency for a wife to claim help from her husband which she would not expect were he in business or in a profession at home is strong and subtle.

· · · · ·

A sensitive conscience about the use of time needs to be maintained. The fact that a missionary is not immediately responsible to some superior as to the use of his time carries with it a serious temptation to laxity in this matter.

· · · · ·

Here in the school, also at Shanghai and similar places, the work must be according to timetable or schedule. There is not so much opportunity to give way to laziness. If someone says, "I feel a bit off color. I don't think I'll go to the office or class this morning"; well, the doctor can test him, and perhaps he says there's nothing wrong. So back to work he has to go. In inland places there is not the same safeguard against this snare. It is easy to waste time. The inland missionary after breakfast may sit down to the newspaper or let the time slip by in another way. But this cannot be done in business life. No, a man hurries off to his job, else he will soon find he is not wanted. I have found the need of much watchfulness and self-discipline in this matter during my years in the interior.

· · · · ·

It is also true that even with a fixed timetable or schedule it is possible to be indolent there too. One can do the work in a slovenly manner without heart or preparation. Then, too, we may be faithful when we are preparing to preach before a crowd; but when it is just teaching half a dozen Chinese, I found the need of watchfulness against careless work. May we have grace to do our best every time and all the time.

· · · · ·

When young people first come out, how this one or that one makes an impression by ability, zeal, or personality. It is easy to imagine such and such a one is going to make a great success. But it is wiser to wait and see. Often the unnoticed and less gifted ones by sheer diligence and devotion become the successes.

"Ephraim is as a heifer that loveth to tread out the corn" (Hos. 10:11). Most of us are familiar with the picture of an ox or heifer standing between an altar and a plough with the words, "Ready for either," underneath. This is just what Ephraim, as described by the prophet Hosea, was not. He loved an easy life and a soft piece of work in preference to service that involved real sacrifice and toil. This was the more sad because Ephraim originally was designed for preeminence amongst the tribes, which preeminence, rightly understood, involved special burdens and even sufferings on behalf of others. In the previous history of the tribe there are indications that the claims of this special vocation had in large measure met with an adequate response; so much so that, as time went on, Ephraim became the metropolitan tribe of the ten, its name frequently including the other nine. Declension had not come about all at once. It was due rather to gradual lowering of ideals and of standards, and the giving way to self-indulgence and self-interest in seemingly slight and unimportant things.

That the warning conveyed by these words has a special application to the missionary will hardly be denied. His vocation, more than any, calls for special self-sacrifice and the laying aside of personal and family interests. It demands a supreme measure of devotion, diligence, and concentration of purpose. The missionary's personal habits and the way in which he spends his time are in unusual degree observed by those around him, any inconsistency between his message and his life being noted. It will not avail much, for example, to preach to the Chinese of access to God through the blood of Jesus if they find that there is not access to the missionary himself and his home. That close contact with people of a different civilization often involves trial is true. There is danger lest we should draw back from that contact, thus failing to pay the full price of a truly Christ-like relationship with those around. May we have grace in all these things, like the apostle of old to suffer all things lest we hinder the gospel, thus approving ourselves as his servants.

Love Worked Out in Daily Life

EVERY true Christian wants more love. How does the Lord make us to increase and abound in this love? One way may be by putting alongside of us somebody who very much calls for the exercise of love. You see, it is quite easy if somebody wants to do us a good turn, to be kind to such a one; but it is another matter to have one right alongside who tries you very much, and if you are going to get along at all it has to be by the exercise of love.

I am inclined to think that this is one way in which the Lord increases our love. We pray to him, "Lord, fill me with thy love," and perhaps we have an idea that there will be a warm benevolent feeling floating down towards us of love toward everybody. Well, praise the Lord when we have that! But ah, you have got to work it out in the daily life! The Spirit of God shows us the beauty of love, we rejoice in it, but it has to be worked out like algebraic problems. And it is so important to see that before the Lord can entrust us with a lot of people, he has got to see how we can love a few.

· · · · ·

One reason why there are not more converts gathered in is that we fail right here. The Lord puts alongside of us perhaps a babe, a babe in Christ, a vexatious sort of person, one who walks along the natural plane, carnal, self-willed, self-opinionated, self-conceited. That babe is in Christ. What are we going to do? We can learn to love that person. I am sure you will agree with me that it is absolutely essential in these matters of relationship with individuals that we win through on the side of love. It is a tremendous fight sometimes. Let us not be defeated here.

· · · · ·

You remember what it says in the book of Proverbs, "He that is slow to anger is better than the mighty; and he that ruleth his spirit than he that taketh a city." We want to take a city – we would like to see New York with many converts gathered in. The Word of God says to rule your spirit is a greater thing than to take a city. If you are longing to go to Africa or India, how about your spirit – do you rule it? It says a man who does not rule his spirit is like a city with all the walls down. The passions go in and out of him just as they like.

· · · · ·

We must not be surprised, if we are earnestly seeking after love, if he permits us to be tried in some fierce way that cuts to the quick, by somebody that goes against the grain. And the trial keeps on. It is not just as a storm soon over, but going on and on.

I believe that the Lord is looking at us all the time, and if we fight through by faith in Christ, although it is a sore conflict, then we are "made partakers of the love of Christ" more fully. We are made partakers of Christ if we hold fast the beginning of our confidence firm unto the end. That is a great principle. It applies right through the Christian life in many different ways. It applies to salvation at the outset and goes on to the end. Then the Lord says, "Yes, this dear child of mine, through my grace, has won through; he has loved that babe in Christ, that carnal one that I put alongside him, and so I can entrust him with much more."

If you fail to love one, you will certainly fail to love others. It is so easy to say, "People are so trying. I should get along so nicely, and grow in grace so much more, if only So-and-so were not rubbing up against me." But So-and-so is the greatest means of grace you have. It means suffering. Let us remember, friends, that the taking of cities to come depends on these things. It means being delivered unto death, but our future usefulness depends upon it.

Widening Love

It has been well said that, in order to have the highest quality of love, it is necessary to love a great many people. On reflection, the truth of this is apparent. The love of an individual, for instance, who simply cares for himself and has little or no thought and interest in others, is obviously of a meager, not to say undesirable quality. Again, love which is contracted within the circle of family ties and interests, or of our own church, is in danger of being tainted with the same vice of selfishness. Whilst it is true that every Christian has the duties of his own particular sphere to the fulfillment and care of which the individual concerned necessarily and rightly must devote the main part of his time and energy; yet it is of vital importance that each one of us should maintain and cultivate a prayerful, sympathetic interest towards God's people and God's work everywhere. We must be careful to carry out the injunction of our Lord to his disciples to lift up their eyes and look on the fields; otherwise, the words of the old adage, "Out of sight, out of mind," will speedily become true in our case.

• • • • •

It is of practical importance for each one of us to be on our guard against the natural tendency to become contracted in our sympathies. We need, rather, by a definite, prayerful directing of our minds and attention to the larger spheres outside our immediate surroundings, to widen as well as deepen our practical interest in the work and welfare of others. May it not be that, in some cases, one reason for lack of progress in the Christian life is failure in conforming to this scriptural condition of loving "all saints."

To All Men

"LET us not be weary in well-doing, for in due season we shall reap if we faint not. As we have therefore opportunity, let us do good unto all men" (Gal. 6:9-10).

That it is easy to grow weary in well-doing most people have found by experience; and this is perhaps especially true in respect of doing good unto all men. There are those who respond to our advances; who appreciate what we do for them and are grateful for it; in the case of such it is not difficult to continue seeking their good. Too often, however, we meet with hardness of heart, ingratitude, and even, in some cases, contempt and dislike from those whose welfare we have at heart. In such circumstances, mere natural benevolence and kindness of heart are not sufficient to prevent our becoming disheartened and, it may be, embittered. In the words of the text, we are tempted to "faint" and so to fail in carrying out the necessary condition of reaping a harvest from our sowing. Nothing short of the love of God continually shed abroad in our hearts by the Holy Ghost will avail us here.

· · · · ·

In the opening passage of the epistle to the Hebrews, we are told how God, notwithstanding the rejection of his repeated efforts for the good of men through the ministry of the prophets during preceding ages, "hath in these last days spoken unto us by his Son." That is to say, just when we might have expected him to abandon his efforts for man's blessing and to deal in final judgment, we find that the Lord, so far from giving up, exhibits still greater love towards those who have been slighting his goodness. The Lord Jesus, when on earth, manifested the Father amongst men and told his disciples that they, too, in their measure, were to make him known, not merely by telling forth with their lips the story of redemption, but by exhibiting in their own persons and conduct the very kindness and forbearance of God towards men. In other words, they were to be the channels or vessels in and through which Christ would exhibit his grace, his love and his long-suffering. As the apostle Paul puts it in another of his writings, their gospel was to be "not in word only, but in deed and in truth."

In accordance with this great principle, we find in the epistles several specific injunctions regarding the relation of the Christian to his fellow men. We are commanded, for example, to "honor all men"; to offer "prayers and thanksgiving for all men"; to be "gentle unto all"; "long-suffering toward all." It must ever be borne in mind that the spiritual value and fruitfulness of our work, individually and as a Mission, depends, for the most part, upon the nature of our contact and intercourse with the people around us. Is it Christ-like, or is it more or less controlled by the self-life? May the Lord grant us grace to be true witnesses to him.

Selected Writings

D. E. Hoste's contributions to *China's Millions* were no ordinary devotional leading articles. They bore the unmistakable mark of the profound thinking that characterized him and dominated his decisions. To read these articles is not only to gain an insight into the practical out-working of spiritual laws, but to understand, in a deeper way, the man himself.

Jonathan's Robe

"Jonathan stripped himself of the robe that was upon him, and gave it to David" (1 Sam. 18:4).

The significance of this action on the part of Jonathan can only be fully appreciated by consideration of the events in his life as recorded in the previous chapters of this book. It will be remembered that in the fourteenth chapter is given the account of one of the most remarkable deliverances ever wrought on behalf of Israel. The Philistines had invaded the country in overwhelming force; the armies of Israel were not only completely subdued and disorganized, but were even deprived of their weapons of war by the conquerors. Never, perhaps, in the history of the chosen race do we find them in a more hopeless and humiliating position than that described in the closing part of the thirteenth chapter. So complete was the disarmament that swords remained only in the hands of Saul the king and of Jonathan, his son. Then follows the wonderful story of how, through the faith and courage of the young prince, the whole aspect of affairs was completely changed in the course of a few hours. The country was rid of the presence of its hated oppressors, their yoke broken, and the national honor and independence once more secured. It can be seen at once that Jonathan must have been the hero of the hour, and that the eyes of the whole nation must have been turned in gratitude and loyal devotion towards him. A great and glorious career lay before him. He was heir to the throne and had proved himself worthy to occupy it, whilst the hopes of Israel were fixed upon him.

Soon afterwards a sudden and great change takes place. In an hour of threatened national danger and dishonor, another individual unexpectedly achieves a great victory, and at once the enthusiasm both of the army and of the people at large becomes centered upon David. This was the crisis of Jonathan's life. What was to be his attitude towards the one who had suddenly surpassed and overshadowed him? There could be no more searching test of character. It is not easy for anyone to find his prospects of influence and usefulness interfered with by the appearance of another upon the scene. The natural spirit of self-assertion is too apt to rebel against what seems to be a usurpation of one's own rights. Alas! how easily the deadly seeds of jealousy and unkindness germinate in the heart under such circumstances.

Judged by the ordinary standards of the world, the career of Jonathan might be said to have ended prematurely in failure, and with the splendid prospects of his early manhood unrealized. Estimated in the light of God's Word, its value and significance are far otherwise. The lesson which it teaches us is, perhaps, best expressed in the words of our Lord: "He that loseth his life shall save it." The real worth and completeness of a career cannot be reckoned in the light of its outward circumstances. Apparent failure may mean the deepest and most lasting success. In other words, it is the spirit in which the life is lived which is the essential point. It is characteristic of the Holy Scriptures to be silent concerning the inward conflicts through which Jonathan must have passed in connection with his relationship with David. It is enough to know that he was a man of like passions with ourselves and that therefore he must have realized fully and keenly all that the acceptance of David as God's appointed man involved to himself. It would be a complete mistake to regard Jonathan as a mere weak, sentimental, facile youth for whom the prospects of a great position held no attraction. The account already referred to of the national deliverance wrought by the Lord through him sufficiently shows the fallacy of such a view. No, the secret of Jonathan's action lay in a deep subjection to the will of God, and in the habit of communion with the Lord, which produced in him a humble, unselfish spirit. Hence, when this supreme and searching test of his life came, he met it in a right way.

We who are God's children in the present dispensation are accustomed to regard ourselves as living on a higher plane than did his servants in the Old Testament times, and there is, of course, Scriptural ground for our so doing. And yet, as we contemplate this act of Jonathan's and consider his subsequent relationship with David, may we not take shame to ourselves for our slowness to "let the mind that was in Christ Jesus be in us," and to make ourselves of no reputation in order to make room for the gifts and ministry of others. Let us remember that God's arrangements for the cooperation of his servants in his work will be contrary to the mind of the flesh in each one of us simply because they are in accordance with the mind of Christ. And as the Lord seeks to lead us each one on into a truer and purer fellowship with himself, we shall most certainly find that the path opened before us involves an ever deepening and fuller measure of death to self and self-seeking in its manifold forms. Our relationship with others will be increasingly that of the bond-servant, who is expected to sacrifice himself and his interests on behalf of those whom the Lord appoints him to serve.

It is a solemn truth that any refusal on our part to allow this spirit practically to govern us of necessity means hindrance to the Lord's plans and loss to his work. It is sadly possible to "seek our own" even whilst there may be a considerable measure of honest zeal and devotion to the service of God.

May we all have grace to perceive and loyally to respond to every fresh call which the Master may make upon us to go forward in the path of self-emptying. As we do so, we shall "win him" in ever-increasing measure, and the quality of our life and service will correspondingly improve.

Perseverance in Prayer

"So Ahab went up to eat and drink. And Elijah went up to the top of Mount Carmel" (1 Kings 18:42).

It seems clear from the context that both were right. Ahab had just been restored from years of idolatry; and though by his office he was leader of the nation, he was neither fit nor called to accomplish the final act of their deliverance from famine. That was for the man who through steadfast faith and patient courage in the face of general apostasy had been trained and fitted to be the savior of his people.

Yet some may ask whether, after all, it was really necessary for Elijah, tired and spent as he must have been after the strain of the preceding scenes, to give himself to persistent, importunate prayer until the rain fell. The Lord had said: "Go, show thyself to Ahab and I will send rain upon the earth." At the risk of his life he had obeyed; further, he had turned both king and people from the worship of Baal, thus removing the cause of the famine. Surely, then, it might be said, it was the part of faith to rest upon the promise already given – "I will send rain upon the earth." Not so did the man argue through whom the Lord was effecting his will. He knew that God often gives promises in order that his servants may carry out the conditions of their fulfillment and then by their persevering prayers bring them to pass. Elijah had not forgotten the original message three and a half years before that there was not to be rain but according to his word. Therefore, now that it was morally possible for the rain to fall, he must at all costs give himself to prayer till it came.

Again, he does not simply pray once and then "believe" for the answer; but in the face of repeated delay and discouragement, he keeps on till the answer comes.

We are reminded of the words, "Take heed to the ministry thou hast received in the Lord, that thou fulfill it." Alas! how many victories are just missed, how often deliverance is just not achieved, through shortcoming and failure here.

Amongst other instances, Jericho is a notable one. Here again it might have been argued that the previous explicit statement that the land had been given to Israel rendered the blowing of the rams' horns day after day superfluous. But that was the procedure laid down by the Lord himself.

The experience of Jacob at Peniel teaches the same lesson. The reference in Hosea 12:4 to this incident throws light upon the account in Genesis. "By his strength he was a prince [margin] with God: Yea, he had power over the angel and prevailed: he wept and made supplication unto him." And this went on all night. As the day dawned, the Angel said, "Let me go, for the day breaketh." Would Jacob, weary as he must have been, accept that as a final word of discouragement and denial? His answer came clear and strong, "I will not let thee go except thou bless me." And so he prevailed and was owned by God as a prince.

We think, too, of the woman of Tyre and Sidon who prayed on in the face of the Lord's silence and seeming rebuff, winning from him the words, "Oh woman, great is thy faith."

Again in Acts 12 can we believe that Peter would have been delivered by the angel from prison, but for the fact that "instant and earnest prayer [margin] was made without ceasing of the church to God for him"? To guard against misunderstanding, it must at this point be said clearly that there are various aspects of prayer life and service, of which the foregoing is but one. In this, as in most things touching spiritual life and service, there are dangers from spurious, morbid self-effort, leading sometimes to sad disaster. Moreover, the Word of God gives us instances of quiet, believing prayers, to which answers were granted at once, or delayed, as the case might be.

The foregoing remarks, therefore, are by no means intended as laying down a single rule or method of prayer to the exclusion of others. Prayer, like everything else worth doing, is not easy and therefore needs practice. We become strong in its exercise, not so much by reading books about it – that will help as much as a book on cricket or riding will make a good cricketer or horseman – but by setting ourselves to do it and by steady continuance in it.

Our Lord, in response to the disciples' request for teaching about prayer, gave prominence to importunity. Exactly why may not be easy to determine. Such an inquiry brings us into the realm of the unseen, concerning which our knowledge is but limited – hence the need of caution and reserve in attempting to deal with it. The aspect of prayer as a conflict with evil spiritual powers is, as all students of the Bible know, indicated in more than one place. Perhaps the most striking is in Daniel 9 and 10, in the latter of which the prophet, who with burdened heart had for weeks been seeking the face of God on behalf of Israel, was told that the delay in the answer to his prayer was due to the opposition of hostile spiritual power.

Again, in the well-known passage at the close of Ephesians, we are taught that we do not wrestle with flesh and blood but we do wrestle with evil spirits. This, to a superficial view, may seem inconsistent with the teaching in the early part of the epistle concerning our standing in Christ far above all opposing powers; it is really the complement of it. One thing is certain: the more we wait upon God in intercession, the more will we feel the constraint of the Spirit to do so. The converse is also true; he is easily grieved and hindered in this matter, whether by the sin of sloth and unwillingness for the toil and travail involved, or through the habit of allowing other things to crowd out prayer, or through one-sided interpretations of Scripture that shut out this aspect of revealed truth because seemingly inconsistent with certain others.

It is a serious question whether in the training of workers for the ministry, or in gatherings for the edification of Christians, the vital nature of this ministry of instant, prevailing prayer is enforced as it should be, and sufficient time definitely set apart for its practice. The allowance must, of course, always be made for the fact that in this, as in every other branch of Christian life, the experience of each individual will have its own character and measure.

The subject of persevering, prevailing prayer has been chosen for this meditation because we are convinced that the condition of China, whether as relating to the Christian church and the work of the gospel, or to the country as a whole, depends more upon it than anything else. Whilst we thankfully appreciate all that is being done in faithful, persevering prayer by our friends and fellow-workers both at home and in the field, we believe that more is urgently needed. Is it not possible that by a thoughtful readjustment of the use of our time, some, if not all of us, may be able to accomplish more for God than ever before?

The Harvest of Self-will

"Thorns also and thistles shall it bring forth to thee" (Gen. 3:18).

The above words describe one sure result of discontent with a divinely-appointed limitation, and of self-willed efforts on the part of man to obtain that which was not in the purpose and will of God. He must have fruit, whether forbidden or not; and lo, he finds that he has but obtained a harvest of thorns.

It is to be observed that the fruit of the tree of knowledge of good and evil, which was the subject of the divine prohibition, was not in itself bad or undesirable; on the contrary, it had been created by the Lord and was, therefore, "very good." Whether in course of time our first parents would have been permitted to partake of the fruit it is impossible to say, as the Holy Scriptures are silent on the point. However that may be, the solemn lesson is the same as we contemplate the consequences that flowed from that act of disobedience. It is well to take to heart and constantly to bear in mind the practical application to ourselves of this lesson as we pass through life, and to take heed lest at any time we should grasp at some prospect or some advantage which it is not in the purpose of our heavenly Father for us to possess and enjoy. The question, be it repeated, is not as to the intrinsic goodness or otherwise of a particular object, but rather whether it be God's choice and appointment for us.

Students of Scripture are familiar with the contrast presented between the first Adam and the second in this regard. We find the first placed in a garden and surrounded by all that could minister to his wants and gratify his tastes, one single limitation alone being placed upon him. Our Lord, on the contrary, is led by the Holy Spirit into the wilderness to endure the pangs of hunger and to experience the apparent forgetfulness and neglect of his bodily needs by his heavenly Father. It was his in obedient faith and perfect patience to accept his circumstances of want and privation and to wait patiently until such time as his Father sent relief. We know that the essence of the satanic temptation lay not in any intrinsic wrong attached to the act of turning stone into bread, but in the departure from this attitude, which such an act would involve. The Christian must expect to be confronted with this temptation in one form or another, not once only but many times, as he passes through life; and he needs to recognize that it is no sign of his heavenly Father's displeasure if he too is at times suffered to hunger. For it was, indeed, just after the Lord Jesus had received the testimony that he pleased God that this experience was sent to him.

It is possible in this connection to be a "stony ground hearer," that is, we may at one time honestly and with joy receive the word of this teaching, and yet later on, fail before further temptations brought by new circumstances in life. How important for us so to be walking with God that the senses are exercised to discern between good and evil, and thus be preserved from the allurements that would turn us from the path of the divine will.

For instance, is it not sadly true that many a harvest of "thorns and thistles" has been reaped by sorrowing parents through failure in this important point? The Scriptures record as one of the grievous sins of Israel that "they made their children go through the fire to Moloch"; and may not something of the same iniquity lurk in parents allowing such considerations as social advancement and better prospects in this life unduly to influence them in their arrangements for the education and starting in life of their children, whilst the claims of their spiritual interests are practically given a secondary place?

The action of Joseph in regard to his two sons is a striking instance of a parent observing the will of God and holding fast to it in spite of great temptations in the opposite direction. It was obviously open to Joseph to found a great house in Egypt and start his sons in careers of influence and honor in what was then the dominant power of the world. But we find him bringing them to the feet of Jacob and casting in their lot with the humble, alien shepherds living entirely outside the great world of Egypt. It is noticeable that in Heb. 11:21 the blessing of these sons of Joseph is recorded as the outstanding act of faith in the life of Jacob, showing that he participated with Joseph in the choice thus made.

Again, in regard to the acquisition of wealth, how many have proved that riches are "deceitful"; and how often has the desire for them injured the spiritual life! Not, be it repeated, that wealth in itself is an evil; on the contrary, it may and should be a means of great good. The practical danger is lest the heart become ensnared with the desire for it, and thus it gradually usurp the place which the Lord and his interests should have. The warning conveyed by our Lord himself in his parable of the man who pulled down his barns and built larger, and also the numerous exhortations in the Scriptures to be content with such things as we have, need ever to be born in mind. We may well ponder the words with which our Lord closes the account of this man – esteemed, doubtless, by his fellow men as able and prosperous – but described by God as "a fool," with the added comment, "so is he that layeth up treasure for himself and is not rich toward God." May God give us all grace to be perfectly honest with him about this matter, so that whether in his providence our earthly possessions increase or diminish, we can truly say in the words of the well-known hymn: "Naught that I have my own I call, I hold it for the Giver."

The Folly of Human Preference

"And the Lord said to Samuel, hearken to their voice, and make them a king" (1 Sam. 8:22).

We find in Scripture several instances recorded of the Lord granting the desires of men even though such desires are contrary to his own will. It would seem, indeed, to be a principle of God's moral government that he does not go beyond a certain point in withstanding the self-will of his creatures, at all events during the probationary period of his dealings with them. The circumstances connected with the appointment of Saul, the son of Kish, as the first king of Israel are a notable illustration of this truth. Whether it was the divine purpose ultimately to introduce the monarchical form of government into Israel or not, it is clear that the desire of the people for such a change was not only ill-timed, but that they were actuated by wrong motives in entertaining it. The theocratic order, under which the Lord himself prepared and brought forward a man to be his instrument in the government of his people, was the original divine choice; and their insistence on another order being substituted for it amounted, as we learn from the sacred record, to a virtual rejection of the Lord himself as the head and ruler of the nation. Nevertheless, their request was granted in the words quoted above, and we find that not long afterwards Saul is brought forward and is generally accepted as king. The succeeding chapters of the first book of Samuel recount the sad train of disastrous consequences to Israel resulting from their own impatience and self-will. We may be certain that had they manifested a right spirit, and in an attitude of humility, patience, and self-judgment, waited upon the Lord to make clear his own arrangement for meeting the needs of the nation, events would have taken a very different course. The book of Judges reiterates again and again the gracious truth that in times of national need and disaster, even though brought about by the sin and backsliding of the people, if only they turned with their whole heart to the Lord, he was prepared to undertake their cause and to give them someone chosen and equipped by himself for their deliverance.

As we follow the history of King Saul, we are impressed by the fact that, though he seems to have failed at a comparatively early period of his reign, the divine intervention for his removal was slow in operating. It is true that in purpose he was rejected from the kingdom, and that the man who, in the Divine Providence, was to be his successor, was anointed for the kingly office; nevertheless, long years passed, during which we are told that the Spirit of God had been withdrawn from Saul, and he had been given up to the influence of an evil spirit, thus becoming an incubus and a blight upon the prosperity of his country. The experience of the people of Israel during this lengthened period furnishes an instructive instance of the truth that, when men through impatience and self-will insist upon something which is not God's purpose for them, they will most surely have to eat the fruit of their own doings; and the train of events thus set in motion will have to run its course, sad and fruitful in mischief though it may prove to be. These things are written for our admonition, upon whom the ends of the world are come; and it especially behooves those called to take an active share in the Lord's service to take heed to themselves, lest through carelessness of walk, or neglect of the means of grace, they should gradually get out of touch with God and lose the capacity to perceive his will. Trifling with conscience and lack of full obedience to the Holy Spirit in the personal life of a Christian expose him to the grave danger, either of exhibiting self-will, or at least taking a mistaken course of action in times of testing and perplexity.

The case of the patriarch Abraham in connection with the birth of Ishmael shows us how even the man of eminent faith and obedience may err and commit a mistake fruitful in mischief during succeeding years. It will be remembered how when he perceived that his action was going to result in discord, Abraham sent away Hagar in the hope of thus averting trouble, which was evidently impending over his family. But it was not to be: God himself sent Hagar back. Nor is it difficult to see that, for years afterwards, there were elements of strife and unhappiness in the domestic life of Abraham, the outcome of his failure, in a time of testing, to exercise simple faith and patience as fully as he should have done.

Spiritual Blessing – Its Truest Measure

"With all lowliness and meekness, with long-suffering, forbearing one another in love" (Eph. 4:2).

It will be remembered that in the chapters preceding the above words the apostle has set before us the standing of a believer in Christ, with the boundless blessings attaching to that position, and in the closing passage of the third chapter he reaches, as it were, a climax in the wonderful prayer that we may be strengthened with might by the Spirit in the inner man, that Christ may dwell in our hearts by faith, and that, thus being rooted and grounded in love, we may be able to comprehend with all saints and to know the love of Christ which passeth knowledge, that we may be filled with all the fullness of God.

We might have expected that the writer, having thus set before us the marvelous provisions of divine grace, would go on to exhort us to greater energy and enterprise in the work of God and to bolder and grander schemes for the advancement of his kingdom upon earth, and in this way to walk worthy of our high vocation. The Holy Spirit, however, would have us know that there is something more fundamental, more important, and more pleasing to our heavenly Father than this, i.e. the exercise of humility and love between his children.

We do well to bear in mind that it is in the maintenance of right relationships with our fellow-Christians that the depth and reality of such spiritual blessing as we may have received will be most truly measured and manifested. If we fail here, then we may be sure that there is something seriously defective in the blessing which we think we possess. It is sadly possible, as we are reminded in the thirteenth chapter of the first epistle to the Corinthians, to display much real zeal and capacity in the service of God which, in his sight, are largely of no account because we are not living and dealing with our fellows in a right spirit. We need the fullness and the renewing of the Holy Spirit in order to walk in love and forbearance towards our brethren; and it is the one who humbles himself as a little child who is really greatest in the kingdom of heaven and who will be used to accomplish most in the extension of that kingdom.

It may seem a paradox to say that the need of the graces just referred to is especially great in times of spiritual power and progress. It seems inevitable that at such periods there are always those who tend to cling unduly to the well-tried and hallowed usages of the past; whilst another section is apt to be too hasty and become impatient with what appears to them the unreasonable and groundless conservatism of their brethren. In this way, the unity of Christians, and also the continuity of the work of the Holy Spirit in and through them, are both endangered. Times of transition, therefore, call for the utmost prayerfulness and a full measure of the spirit of mutual consideration and patient regard for each other's views and feelings on the part of the Lord's servants.

We shall find it full of profit to study the example set us by our blessed Master in his relationships with John the Baptist. The Lord Jesus, regarded as a preacher of the kingdom of God, came to introduce something which, in the nature of things, was bound to eclipse and in a real, though not complete sense, to supersede the teaching and influence of his forerunner. We find, however, that he makes his first public appearance as one who publicly owned John the Baptist as a teacher come from God, and by the act of receiving baptism at his hands, taking the position of one of his followers. It was whilst doing this that he received the testimony that his heavenly Father was well pleased with him; and the humility and self-effacement, on his side, of John the Baptist, completes the beautiful picture.

Amongst numerous other instances in the Word of God, we may refer to the manner in which the apostle Peter met the objections of some of the Jewish Christians to his – in their eyes – unlawful intercourse with the Gentile Cornelius. Peter does not stand upon his dignity as an apostle and leader in the church or show resentment and impatience towards his critics. But in a frank and brotherly way he explains to them, in detail, the circumstances; and in this way the threatened danger of breach of unity was averted.

The apostle Paul himself is an outstanding example of similar conduct. There is, and always has been, a species of toleration which, whilst posing under the name of large-hearted charity, is really due to a lax indifference with regard to truth. But with Paul it was far otherwise. Perhaps no man ever had a more clear and intense conviction of the great truths which in a special way characterized his ministry, and no one could have seen more clearly than he the inherent limitations of the type of Christianity prevalent amongst the churches in Judea; yet we find that he left no stone unturned in order to keep on terms of Christian charity and fellowship with them, even though there seems reason to think that some of them misunderstood and misrepresented his teaching. We find him, for instance, encouraging the churches in Greece to subscribe towards the relief of their fellow believers in and around Jerusalem, and with characteristic generosity he reminds his own converts that it is to the Jewish Christians that they owe, under God, the gospel.

May we all so abide in Christ that whether in our strictly personal relationships with fellow Christians, or in discussing with them wider questions of method and usage, we may be governed by the inspired words which we have been considering.

Like-mindedness amongst God's Children

"Now the God of patience and consolation grant you to be like-minded one toward another according to Christ Jesus" (Rom. 15:5).

In these words, the apostle recognizes that like-mindedness amongst God's children is the result of divine power and grace rather than of human effort, however sincere and well-intentioned. His language also implies that the attainment of this like-mindedness will not always be an easy matter, but rather the reverse. God himself is exercising much patience in order to bring men into a state of like-mindedness with himself, and it is this same God of patience who alone can work in us and so secure a similar condition, not only as between himself and his children, but as amongst them in their mutual relationships. Some difficulties in the way of realizing this end may here be referred to.

Much is due to the natural depravity of our hearts, which tends to engender in us a perverse and obstinate spirit holding on to our own point of view and makes us unwilling to admit mistake. Not the least dangerous feature of this tendency is its subtlety. It may frequently operate in our minds and bias our view of things quite unknown to ourselves. A habit may thus be formed of instinctively holding on to our own righteousness and adhering to our own ways and opinions in a spirit that will effectually blind us to anything that may be urged on the other side of the case. We are repeatedly warned in the Holy Scripture against this form of self-deception, and are also taught that it is the poor in spirit and the meek who will be truly taught of God and led into a right and true view of the matters concerning which there may be difference of opinion amongst brethren. "Blessed are the poor in spirit, for theirs is the kingdom of God."

Another frequent hindrance to growth in like-mindedness is to be found in the prejudice resulting from incomplete and one-sided knowledge. It is a common attitude of men in controversy unduly to dwell upon the errors and the weak points in others, without sufficiently taking into account such truth and such goodness and strength of character as they may possess. Unless we are on our guard, it is easy to allow the faults and mistakes of our opponents to blind us to their virtues; whilst, on the other hand, the good points attaching to our own side can equally blind us to its blemishes. In this connection it is instructive to observe the discriminating and comprehensive character of our Lord's estimate of the seven churches, to whom he sends his messages through his servant John, as recorded in the early chapters of the Revelation. His words include generous recognition of all that was praiseworthy in those he was addressing, whilst at the same time not passing over their failures.

Another hindrance to like-mindedness sometimes arises from the irritation and personal feeling excited in the course of discussion. The mutual ascription of unworthy motives and aspersions on the personal character of those between whom differences exist, are, it is to be feared, responsible for more division amongst Christian people than the intrinsic antagonism between the opinions they may severally hold. It would be easy to mention other hindrances, but the foregoing will be sufficient for our purpose of emphasizing our need of the inworking of the God of patience in order to realize like-mindedness.

There is a kind of easy-going agreement with others, the outcome not of genuine charity, but of haziness and laxity in one's own opinions. On the other hand, where there is intensity of conviction and a deep sense of its vital importance, the maintenance of a judicial mind and a patient, charitable attitude towards those who differ from us is often extremely difficult. In this respect the apostle Paul furnishes us with a bright and outstanding example. We know from his own writings that the great truths concerning redemption and the church of God were specially revealed to him, as a vessel chosen to make them known amongst men; and it is quite clear from his writings that his apprehension of these divine mysteries permeated his whole being. How intensely then must he have felt the coldness and apathy with which his teaching was met in some quarters, to say nothing of the suspicion and even opposition shown by certain sections of the Christian community. It is easy to imagine that the temptation sometimes must have come to him with no little strength to cease from the endeavor to maintain fellowship with the churches in Judea, amongst whom his doctrine seems to have made little, if any progress. So far from yielding to this temptation, we find Paul habitually seeking, as opportunity offered, to strengthen the ties between himself and his brethren at Jerusalem. Is there a famine in Judea? We find him exhorting the Gentile churches to collect money, and he devotes time and care to seeing that these contributions are safely sent to those in need of them. He seems to have realized that the manifestation of practical kindness will often go much further to disarm prejudice and overcome opposition than the most dexterous use of logic and other weapons drawn from the armory of the controversialist.

This brings us to the second expression employed in our text as descriptive of God, namely, the God "of consolation." This latter word in the original conveys the idea of the ministry of the Paraclete, the one who will stand by another to strengthen, support, and comfort in the manifold trials of life. In order to act thus towards those who differ from us, there is, indeed, need of divine grace in the heart. We are not only to bear with what we conceive to be the mistakes and opposition of others; we are, as we have opportunity, to be actively kind towards them, to stand by them in their difficulties. By so doing, we shall often find that their hearts and their minds have become opened in a way that would otherwise be quite impossible.

Again as those who differ from us perceive that our minds are open to receive, with respect and consideration, such facts and arguments as they may be led to bring forward, it will become easier for them to adopt a similar attitude towards ourselves. If, on the other hand, our minds are virtually closed against the possible reception of further light, this will inevitably react upon those whom we are endeavoring to influence. It is true of us all that we only know in part, and it is through practical willingness to profit by the ministry of the Holy Ghost through others that we shall be led into an apprehension of the truth at once clearer and more comprehensive than before. We need to subject ourselves the one to the other in the fear of Christ. The opposite attitude, which, in effect, says to our brother, "I have no need of thee," and which engenders more or less contempt and impatience towards their arguments, will certainly result in loss of light to ourselves and loss of power to minister to our brethren in respect of matters under discussion. It is well to wait patiently for one another and to cultivate a sincerely teachable spirit that is willing to learn from others. Thus, and thus alone, will God's people be brought into a like-mindedness that is "according to Christ Jesus."

"Aaron the Saint of the Lord"
Psalm 106:16

The word "saint" as applied to Aaron in the text quoted above means "dedicated, holy," the reference probably being to his office as the high priest of Israel. There is much that is instructive for us, at the present time, in the inspired account of Aaron's appointment and the circumstances connected with it, as recorded in the twenty-eighth and thirty-second chapters of Exodus. In the former chapter the commandment of the Lord to Moses to set apart Aaron and his sons to the priestly office is followed by a detailed statement of the method of the appointment, and of the robes and vestments to be worn by them. Other passages give equally careful and detailed instructions regarding their duties and functions.

1

It would be difficult to exaggerate the high and holy character of these functions, or their far-reaching and vital importance as touching the maintenance of the whole congregation, as well as individual Israelites, in their covenant relationship and communion with Jehovah, which facts carry with them obvious implications as to the need of high and holy character in those selected for the office. And yet it is plain from the two passages already mentioned that at the very time that the Lord was giving Moses the instructions contained in the twenty-eighth chapter of Exodus, Aaron was exhibiting his weakness and instability in the episode narrated in the opening part of the thirty-second chapter. The people, demoralized by the prolonged, and to them unaccountable absence of Moses, gave way to panic; and Aaron, yielding to their clamor for some substitute for their apparently lost leader, makes them a golden calf. Surely, it might with reason be said, his unfitness to be high priest became evident just in time to prevent an unsuitable appointment. Yet we find that, as a matter of fact, that appointment was proceeded with, and that on the whole, Aaron, notwithstanding some faults and errors, did well in it. From which may be learned the possibility of forming wrong estimates of others through giving undue weight to their defects and weaknesses.

It is not always easy rightly to appraise the conduct or misconduct of others. To do so calls for a knowledge of their antecedents and a just appreciation of the significance of a given action in the light of those antecedents. In the case of Aaron, for instance, it was essential to bear in mind that, through long association, both he and the children of Israel were familiar with and, it may even be, had to some extent participated in the calf worship of Egypt. We know from the Scripture that, whilst still in Canaan, the use of the teraphim was not uncommon amongst the Israelites. Many of them were, in fact, only emerging from a habit of mind and of practice more or less idolatrous. Hence the setting up of the calf, wicked as it was, represented a lapse into former ways at a moment of great strain and testing due to the disappearance of the man who, by divine appointment, was not only their leader but also the medium of communication between them and God. They had not yet attained to the capacity of a direct and immediate trust in him, apart from such an intermediary.

2

Further, the very preeminence of Moses meant a relative insignificance and lack of influence for Aaron. This, it would seem, was the first time he was left in charge of the people for any considerable time; and there is not ground for much surprise, if as the days and weeks passed and the general uneasiness and alarm at length culminated in open panic, he proved unable to grip and control the crisis. Few things are more difficult and it may be added more uncommon than for an individual to withstand a strong outbreak of popular feeling.

Another reason why, notwithstanding his failure, Aaron was made high priest, is that Moses, the man of spiritual vision and strong faith, was to stand by him and strengthen his hands. God gives grace and spiritual power to one man in order that he may by his faith, his prayers, and his service, strengthen and uphold others. It is easy to be selfish in our desires for and our choice of fellow workers; we long for the relief and satisfaction of having by us strong and gifted ones, and shrink from the trial involved in cooperation with the unstable, the faulty and spiritually unintelligent. And yet to yield to this temptation may mean that we lose the very ones who, had we fulfilled our ministry of patient, loving cooperation, would have grown into leadership.

3

How did our Lord get his apostles, who in due time built up and extended the church? We know it was by patiently bearing with them in their lack of insight, their unbelief, their pride, their hardness of heart, their instability and other faults. More than that, he not only bore with them, but he trusted them with power and with ministry, sending them forth as his accredited representatives to the house of Israel. Above all, he constantly prayed for them. We may say with reverence that he had the courage, the faith, the hope regarding his disciples, which are amongst the most essential qualities of a great leader. The Bible gives instance after instance of men unpromising enough at first, who subsequently developed into great servants of God by being trusted to bear burdens, face dangers, make decisions, and endure hardness. True, they sometimes stumbled and fell under their trials. But as the Proverb says: "A just man falleth seven times, and riseth up again."

It is to be feared that many whom the Lord would have used in due time in his service have been lost to the church through the failure of those concerned to perceive and appreciate undeveloped possibilities in men, and so being repelled by faults and weaknesses which under wise, sympathetic influence and a spirit of appreciation, they would have grown out of. It is possible to become stereotyped, narrow, and critical in our judgment about others, especially the young and immature, and so fail in one of the most essential qualities of leadership. A Chinese proverb says: "The good ruler is able to make use of men." In other words, he can perceive and find scope for the particular faculties of various kinds of men, notwithstanding their limitations and ineptitudes in some directions. He recognizes, indeed, that the possessions of one kind of power and gift generally involves lack of some other kinds. You cannot bore a hole with a good hammer or drive home a nail with a fret-saw.

4

And so in Scripture we are urged to consider one another to provoke to love and good works. The opposite spirit which makes a man impatient or contemptuous of those built on different lines from himself is a sure sign of a small nature and of unfitness for wide influence and usefulness. The paradox is true that the really great man perceives something superior to himself in every other man; and seeks to turn it to account for the common good.

"The Grace of God"

"By the grace of God I am what I am: and his grace which was bestowed upon me was not in vain" (1 Cor. 15:10).

1

These words seem to indicate the possibility that the grace of God bestowed upon us may be in vain. And if so, why? It is very important, if I may venture to say so, to get at the root of this matter. Many people will tell us – and I am afraid that I have said it myself from time to time – "Well, I have some defect of temperament, or bodily weakness, or something of that kind, and that is why I have made such a poor success of my life as a Christian and a servant of God."

But is that really the reason? It seems to me that the Bible does not teach so. Our weakness, our sinfulness, our foolishness, are opportunities for the grace of God. We will never admit that they are too much for the grace of God. We want to take a right attitude towards the grace of God. I see more and more, as I look back over my Christian life and service, that the radical cause of weakness and inconsistency and instability and failure has been simply that I have not accepted what the Scripture says the grace of God is to me, and for me, and in me. It is simply unbelief that is the root of this.

Oh, how much we may hinder the grace of God by self-effort! It is utterly wrong to say that we hinder the grace of God by, say, a bad temper, or foolish judgment, or being very weak – perhaps a weak kind of a man – or being very strong, or being very conceited. Those things do not hinder the grace of God. The grace of God is meant for those things. Therefore, if we go harping on that as the cause of our failure it simply shows that we are ignoring the grace of God. Is not that sound? Is not that true? It is a sin to do it.

Let us all afresh believe what is revealed to us as the grace of God in Christ: that we are in Christ, that Christ is our life, that we are made "accepted in the beloved." Do you really believe that, or are you looking to yourself, and thinking, "Oh well, I am so unstable," or "I am so unsatisfactory, and oh dear, I get so slack in my Christian life, and I am always backsliding a bit and tumbling over?" If so, you are treating the matter in a radically wrong and hopeless way. That is the way to frustrate the grace of God.

2

You remember that that was the great thing the apostle was contending with in writing to the Galatians. "Christ, yes, but it must be Christ plus something else." That is what those people were after, you remember; but the apostle said, "No, it is Christ alone. It is not a question of what you are at all, or what I am. We are poor sinners through and through." According to our make-up, our education, our surroundings, the sin works out in varying ways. But I do want to impress this on my dear friends and fellow workers, and on everyone who reads these words: Do not let us frustrate the grace of God any longer. Let us accept it; let us believe it. The apostle lays these things down not as some sort of attainment of higher Christian life, but as fundamental, as rudimentary, as the normal Christian life – namely, the life in Christ.

I do feel, as I look back, that that has been the one cause of such failure as there has been in my life; and I want, God enabling me, to press it home on my brethren and sisters. Let us take up a Christian attitude toward Christ. What is that? Simply trusting him, simply counting on him and accepting it that we are filled full in him. The life of trust, that is the normal Christian life. I believe that in the spiritual life you can get into bad habits just as much as you can with your body and your mind. These young people, therefore, in that regard, are better placed than are some of us older ones. Beware of the bad habit of looking at yourself and saying, "But I am so weak." That is not humility, you know. Humility has done with self. It is occupied with Christ; it is occupied with facts. I believe that it is dishonoring to God, to Christ, to be talking about ourselves at all. "Not I, but Christ."

The other day at Cromer I was sitting with a friend at one of those C.S.S.M. services, and the friend who was preaching had a picture of a whole lot of things supposed to be between an individual and the Savior, Christ. One of them was "I," and my friend said to me "Yes, it is 'I,' but it is not the sort of 'I' with all my weaknesses. It is 'I' with self-effort. It is this good 'I' that says 'I have to supplement Christ a little. I have to be perhaps trusting in my praying, or my Bible reading, or in resolutions,'" or something of that kind; as though the fruit, the life, the power came partly from us. But it does not. The fact of the matter is that our own apprehension of the gospel is so imperfect. We want a more simple, direct apprehension and acceptance of the gospel of the grace of God, not only in respect of the guilt of sin, Christ bearing our sins in his own body on the tree, but of the simple fact that he of God is made unto us all we need.

3

I grant you that the apostle in this particular sentence was referring, partly at any rate, to his own ministry, and so on; and of course each of us has a different ministry, has different gifts and so forth. But what I believe is so fundamental to this great missionary work is not that; but it is one's personal experience of the grace of God. It is a sin of unbelief for me to be looking at myself. I want to lay that on myself. We have no business to do it. We all know how the apostle says in the simplest way what he has done, and how he has been delivered from sin, and how he has been kept. Why? Some men would say, "What an egotistical man he is. He tells us about what he has done, and how he has walked holily, justly, and unblameably. Surely a little humility would keep him from referring to that?" Not at all, because Christ had done it. He gloried in Christ, "my Savior." "He," said he, "is my Savior."

Oh, that we who are entrusted with this message may accept the reality for which the message stands, and keep believing! "Keep believing" about the Lord. Not, of course, about oneself. When I am most earth-bound, and most bereft of any feelings of love, or power, or wisdom of any sort or kind, and just like a dry stick, I have to "keep believing." That is the one thing I have to do. My faith and hope are to be in God that raiseth the dead – that is what he wants. I am just nothing. "Nothing in my hand I bring; simply to thy cross I cling." It is like that all the way along. Just take Christ as your life.

I remember so well dear Mr. Hudson Taylor at one of our Saturday prayer meetings in Shanghai in 1898. He was pretty weak in body, and tired and wearied in mind. He was speaking to us and he took that first verse or two of the twenty-seventh Psalm: "The Lord is my light and my salvation; whom shall I fear?" Every man, woman, and child may say that if he or she likes. It is the free gift of God – Christ the Bread from heaven. Wonderful, is it not? "He that hath the Son hath life." How can I have him except I believe? It is just that. Believing I receive.

Then you know the next word: "The Lord is the strength of my life; of whom shall I be afraid?" It is not because you feel it. More and more I see that as we go on in the Christian life the Lord very often does not want to give us the sense of his presence or the consciousness of help. There again Mr. Taylor once helped me very much. We were talking about guidance. He said how in his younger life things used to come so clearly, so quickly, to him; "but," he said, "now as I have gone on and God has used me more and more I seem often to be like a man going along in a fog. I do not know what to do." Of course as you get older and the wear and tear of things tells upon you, you are rather like that, sometimes. Naturally, people vary.

The Lord loves a man who trusts him. That is all he wants. He does not "take pleasure in the legs of man." Be willing to say, "I am a poor little miserable thing, nothing"; and then, if people walk over you, never mind. "Thou hast caused men to ride over our heads." They walked over Jesus the Son of God and put him on the cross, and he was obedient.

4

This is the message which I believe God has given me for you: Get the gospel right into your heart; receive it and believe it. Do not think that you can mend matters by your efforts. I used to talk to people and say, "You must be humble. You must try to live lovingly one with another. You must try to adapt yourself to the Chinese. Be diligent and do not get lazy." Well, those things all have their place. But I believe, for myself, and so I pass it on to other people, that we must trust. That is all you can do, and all he wants you to do. Have faith and hope in God, and then trust him about other people.

Hope in God concerning the poor weak Christians, concerning the backsliders, concerning the people who are going all wrong. I believe that God wants us not only to have faith for ourselves but to have faith and hope and charity for a whole lot of other people. I see it more and more. Now, Lord, I am going to hope in thee about these things, about these people. Do not give up hope. "Love hopeth all things." When you are out there among the people, and badly treated, and when the Christians disappoint you, hope in God. The apostle writing to these

Corinthians who were such a poor lot and who treated him so shabbily, says, "I rejoice therefore that I have confidence in you in all things." Why? Because he knew the Lord. He had confidence in the Lord concerning them.

This is a very simple word, very rudimentary; but we want to believe it. We are greatly distressed about people giving up the faith, and well we may be; but have we let it slip sometimes in practice? The apostle says that he was "not ashamed of the gospel of Christ" – not because it was the best, the most reasonable explanation of things around him and such a wonderful system, no, but because it was the power of God to salvation, and he knew it himself. "The kingdom of God is not in word, but in power." Oh I want more simply to trust in the Lord Jesus Christ and be saved, counting on him as the normal thing. We are blessed "with all spiritual blessings in heavenly places in Christ."

First Things First

"Make me thereof a little cake first" (1 Kings 17:13).

In the chapter from which the foregoing words are selected we find that the famine, primarily intended as a judgment upon apostate Israel, is also the means of furthering the spiritual training of God's true servant Elijah. He, too, is called to share in the general straightness, and thereby experiences as never before the faithfulness and power of God in supplying his needs. Nor is the Lord confined to one method in caring for his servant. As soon as the brook Cherith has dried up, the miraculous feeding by ravens comes to an end, and the prophet is sent to the very country whence the worship of Baal had come, there to be dependent on the bounty of a poor widow, herself on the point of starvation. And so, throughout the whole period of the famine, we find that Elijah is kept in daily and hourly dependence on God. To him, as a man of like passions with ourselves, it would, speaking after the manner of men, have been easier if the Lord had in some way provided an abundant store for the prophet's use, sufficient to last him till the rain fell. It is, however, in the school of constant dependence and prolonged testing of faith and patience that the type of character is formed which is fitted to be God's instrument in the widespread manifestation of his power and grace. Let us not be surprised, therefore, if we, too, find that some divinely provided source of comfort and supply gradually dries up in the same way as the brook Cherith did. As Elijah saw the stream growing smaller and smaller, he must have been tempted sometimes to question and doubt about the future; nor did the Lord tell him how he was to be fed until the brook had actually disappeared. May all of us have grace, under similar experiences, to maintain that quiet confidence and patient trust in our heavenly Father which are pleasing and glorifying to him! It may be that our own health, or that of someone who for long has been a strength and comfort to us, is gradually failing, and we do not see from whence other help is to come. Or it may be that in other ways our resources are getting less. In whatever form the trial may come, let us not forget that he who cared for Elijah is in very truth our God today; and he is watching to see whether we can wholly trust him and learn "in whatsoever state we are, therewith to be content."

It was probably a startling surprise to Elijah to find that the one chosen for his support dwelt in the dark regions of Tyre and Sidon, given up to the worship of Baal. God has his own in unlooked-for quarters. This woman reminds us of that other woman of Tyre and Sidon who was commended by the Lord Jesus for her great faith. It was indeed a bold and unusual request which the prophet, suddenly appearing as a complete stranger, made of her; and right nobly did she respond to it. How easy and natural would it have been for her to have resented the seeming presumption of this stranger and angrily repudiated his claim upon her care. We are reminded of the words of the apostle concerning the Macedonian Christians, of whom it is said that "their deep poverty abounded unto the riches of their liberality."

It will be helpful to us to let our minds dwell on the words, "for me first." It is in circumstances such as those in which the widow was placed that the Lord proves his servants to see whether their profession of loving him first and best of all is genuine or not. It is well to bear in mind that the laying up of treasure in heaven does not depend upon our having large means at our disposal; it depends upon the proportion of our means which we give to the Lord and his work. The Lord Jesus, in speaking of the widow with her two mites having given "more than they all," was not simply speaking of its moral value in the sight of God, but of its actual amount in the bank of heaven. The words, "Many that are first shall be last, and the last first," may ultimately be found to have an application to this matter of giving.

Again, is it not true that the proportion in which the Lord's steward gives to the various objects claiming his help should be regulated by the principle contained in these words, "for me first"? All will agree, for example, that it is the duty, as well as privilege, of a Christian man to contribute to the relief of the poor and needy in the community in times of special scarcity; and in so doing he, in a real way, may be said to give to the Lord. And yet there may be a danger lest the money given in this way be taken from gifts which in ordinary times go in other directions, rather than from the amount usually devoted to personal expenditure; in other words, that the ordinary objects of an individual's gifts, rather than the individual himself, are taxed in order to meet special claims. May every child of God ever remember him who on the cross put us first, and now pleads that we should do the same for him, whether in respect of our means, our time, our strength, or the whole disposal of our lives!

"And Timothy Our Brother"

2 Corinthians 1:1

The apostle Paul furnishes a signal instance of a man who, by birth and training, seemed very unlikely to be able to associate happily with people brought up outside of his own national and religious sphere. And yet, through the triumph of God's grace in him, he maintained, through many years, loving and sympathetic fellowship with a large number of individuals differing greatly, not only from himself, but also from each other. As we look at him before his conversion, with all the religious and national bigotry and pride of a Pharisee, and then contemplate his relations with every class and condition of men, as represented in the Roman Empire of his day, we are constrained to magnify the grace of God in his servant. He seems to have combined, in a remarkable degree, a deep and abiding sense of the fact that he was a man chosen and set apart for a special and most honored ministry, for which he had been endowed with manifold gifts, together with a sweet humility of heart and mind, and a generous appreciation of the gifts and possibilities of usefulness in his brethren. He was signally free from a selfish concern lest by trusting others with responsibility his own influence should be diminished or overshadowed. He seems, indeed, to have lost sight of himself and his own career as being in themselves an end at all. He saw that he only existed as a means to the profit and up-building of others; hence in his service he did not seek his own, but the things which are Jesus Christ's. It was the possession of this spirit which enabled him, when necessary, to vindicate his God-appointed position without the taint of self-assertion and pride.

In this connection the relation of the apostle with his younger colleague Timothy is full of instruction. The latter quite as much held the position of a learner from the apostle as that of a colleague with him, and yet we find that the Holy Spirit leads Paul, when writing some of his epistles, to associate Timothy with himself as the joint author of the letter. He was careful to give him honor and recognition as his colleague before those amongst whom they were laboring. Nor did the fact that his gifts and experience far exceeded those of his younger brother ever make him despise or ignore him and leave him out of account in their common work.

Experience shows that it is often easier to cherish feelings of Christian love for those who may be separated from us by distance than towards those with whom we are constantly and closely associated. This is, no doubt, largely due to the fact that the fall of man has not only affected his spiritual and moral condition, but has also given rise to sad defects both of mind and temperament. Hence, even where through divine grace there may be true love to God and an honest desire to do right, there are often personal idiosyncrasies more or less trying to others affected by them. An individual may, for instance, occasion much difficulty to his companions by hasty and rash conduct; another may be a source of annoyance through undue timidity and vacillation. Again, differences in point of view and in personal habits, due to previous training and education, are apt sometimes to cause strain between fellow Christians. Without discussing here how far these defects of temperament may be eliminated by the indwelling and fullness of the Holy Spirit, we would direct attention to the fact that these very elements in our relationships with others, which at first sight seem to be a hindrance, are intended to promote our growth in grace and our capacity for usefulness in the Lord's service.

How we need practically to bear in mind the truth that it is by that which "every joint supplieth" that the Spirit of God will accomplish his ministry on behalf of the body. No man, however important, can say to another: "I have no need of thee." It is easy, whilst not saying this in so many words, yet in effect to show that we do not consider ourselves dependent upon the cooperation and prayerful judgment of brethren. We need to take heed lest we despise "the least of these little ones." The writer remembers being told in his youth that young men needed to guard against self-conceit, as this was a failing to which they were prone. This, no doubt, was true of the young men of that time; but as years have passed, the question has sometimes presented itself whether those of us who are now older do not need to guard against a still more unpardonable form of conceit, which renders us unable to appreciate and profit by the powers and views of our juniors. Let us remember that the first recorded words of our Lord to his newly-made disciples were: "Blessed are the poor in spirit, for theirs is the kingdom of heaven." Again, in the first epistle to the

Corinthians it is written that "if any man thinks that he knoweth anything, he knoweth nothing yet as he ought to know." Whilst experience in the Lord's work is intended to be, and. should be, a great blessing, it is possible for it, unless accompanied with true humility, to become a hindrance, as it may prevent a man from assimilating new thought, which really represents the mind of God in regard to a new situation.

The importance of this lesson being learned by Christians at the present time can scarcely be overrated. Unless what may be called the grace of colleagueship is cultivated, the growth and development of the Lord's work is sure to be sadly hindered if not entirely stopped. As Chinese Christians are raised up to take a share in the work of the ministry, the practical observance by missionaries of the foregoing principles becomes a matter which is vital to the progress and unity of the work.

May all those who have at heart the building up of God's church in that country give this important subject a place in their prayers and intercessions.

Some Missionary Motives

"For this we know, that no whoremonger, nor unclean person, nor covetous man, who is an idolater, hath any inheritance in the kingdom of Christ and of God. Let no man deceive you with vain words, for because of these things cometh the wrath of God upon the children of disobedience" (Eph. 5:5-6).

The view is held in some quarters, at the present time, that the motives for missionary work which operated in the past have been superseded by others, the outcome of new conditions in the world. That these conditions have to some extent given rise to fresh motives, or have added emphasis to old ones, is true.

It is undeniable that a certain measure of interest in missions has, during recent years, spread widely into quarters where previously they were regarded either with indifference or actual dislike. The dissemination of information by means of conferences, literature, study circles and other agencies is something for which we should be truly thankful. Never before have there been utterances, both by ecclesiastical leaders and by representative bodies, so frankly recognizing the duty of the church to place the evangelization of all peoples in the very forefront of her aims and activities.

All this, whilst affording encouragement, carries with it a grave danger unless there is a corresponding growth in actual service and gifts on behalf of missions. We refer to the great moral principle that failure to respond to fresh light and opportunity incurs the judgment of being given up to a deeper darkness than before. To borrow a figure from the Holy Scriptures, the leaves of profession are one thing, the fruit of performance is another. Further, may we not, without unduly stretching the analogy, say that the position of the church at the present time in regard to missions bears a resemblance to that of the fig tree to which our Lord, when hungry, was attracted by the profusion of its foliage. From this point of view, it must be admitted that the motive of spiritual self-preservation should arouse us as never before to exertions for the spread of the gospel.

We venture to think that the present neglect and indifference on the part of numbers of Christians in regard to the great missionary enterprise may largely be ascribed to a widespread ignoring, if not virtual denial, of certain truths taught in the Scriptures, which truths, if believed, furnish the most cogent reasons for greater zeal and self-denial in seeking to spread the gospel amongst all nations. It is to one of these truths that we wish now to direct attention.

The passage in the epistle to the Ephesians quoted at the head of these lines is but one amongst many references of a similar import, which occur both in the Old and New Testaments. We find, for example, in the first chapter of the epistle to the Romans and the eighteenth verse, the following words: "The wrath of God is revealed from heaven against all ungodliness and unrighteousness of men." Again, the following words occur in the sixth chapter of first Corinthians, verses nine and ten:

"Know ye not that the unrighteous shall not inherit the kingdom of God? Be not deceived, neither fornicators, nor idolaters, not adulterers, nor effeminate, nor abusers of themselves with mankind, nor thieves, nor covetous, nor drunkards, nor revilers, nor extortioners, shall inherit the kingdom of God"; further, in the fifth chapter of Galatians, verses 19 to 21, we find words of a like nature. The whole tenor of the teaching of the Bible on this gravely important subject is that, whilst men are never condemned for ignorance of truth, the opportunity for learning which has been withheld from them, they are held strictly accountable for a right use of such light as has been granted them. It is to be feared that in the reaction against one-sided, exaggerated teaching of former years, which, in effect, involved men in condemnation for ignorance of that which, so far as they were concerned, it was impossible for them to know, the opposite tendency to minimize, or even deny, any moral guilt on the part of those who have not heard the gospel, not only is responsible for a great deal of absolute indifference in regard to missions, but prejudicially affects the earnestness even of those who are, to some extent, actively interested in them. Superficial thought and loose reasoning, which virtually deny any responsibility on the part of "the heathen," have, we believe, paralyzed the energies of Christians in this enterprise to a greater extent than is generally admitted. The minds of not a few become confused by what is really irrelevant discussion as to how far people who have never read or heard the Scriptures are responsible for the errors which they have imbibed as members of some other system of religious thought, the real point at issue being their conduct in relation to such light as they possess.

Observation of life as it is at the present time makes it clear that in every country, whether professedly Christian or otherwise, there are vast numbers of men who are habitually committing acts such as are described in the passage of Scripture we are considering, that involve disregard of their moral obligation and so incur condemnation. Further, that, as a result of continuance in such conduct, men become enslaved to the power of sin. That is to say, we are confronted, on the one hand, with the overwhelming problem of human guilt, whilst on the other looms, as its awful complement, the dark fact of human bondage to the power of moral evil.

The message of the New Testament to men in such a condition may be described, in very general terms, as of a two-fold nature. First is the declaration of the gospel with its salvation from the guilt and power of sin; there is also the fuller and more definite revelation of the solemn, ultimate issues of continued impenitence. It might, perhaps, be more correct to reverse the order of these two. Throughout the Old and New Testaments we find that appeals to the motive of fear, and warning as to the consequences of persistence in evil, form a prominent part of the divine message to man; and any system of thought and teaching which omits to bring this motive to bear on the consciences of men is radically defective and unsound.

We venture the assertion that, antecedent to a revival of missionary zeal, which shall result in progress at once deep and widespread of the Christian faith, there is need of a revival amongst us of the foregoing doctrines of Holy Scripture.

After all, the Christian revelation deals primarily with the supreme question of man's relation with his Creator, and no amount of earnestness in the effort for the social amelioration of men, valuable and important as this is in its place, can make up for vague and defective views concerning the great doctrines to which allusion has been made in the foregoing remarks. The history of the church teaches that it is the deepest truths which, when faithfully propagated, prove, in the long run, the most fruitful in widest influence for good on society at large.

The Character of Hudson Taylor

Report giving the substance of an Address by D. E. Hoste at Shanghai in 1915.

I should like to allude to a few points in the character of Mr. Hudson Taylor which impressed me personally, and which

I think had something to do with the blessing that God granted to his efforts on behalf of this country.

1. His prayerfulness. He was of necessity a busy man, but he always regarded prayer itself as in reality the most needful and important part of the work. He practically recognized that much time must be spent in seeking God's guidance if a right understanding was to be obtained of the problems and difficulties that confronted him in carrying on the work of the Mission. He knew that in no other way was the power of the Holy Spirit to be obtained for himself and his brethren as they sought to develop the work. I venture on this occasion, not only to impress upon myself, but upon you as well, the importance of our copying him in this respect.

2. Another feature of Mr. Taylor's character was his humility. This was manifested in his readiness to listen to and carefully weigh the opinions of his brethren, including those younger than himself. He was always prepared to assimilate thought from others, and herein lay one secret of his successful leadership. By taking counsel with his brethren, he avoided the danger of mental isolation, which is apt to overtake men as they grow older; and his mind retained its youth and elasticity. He maintained a similar attitude towards Chinese Christians and workers whom he recognized, as in some important respects, better able than himself to form a wise judgment and do efficient work amongst their own people.

3. Again, Mr. Taylor was possessed by intense zeal for the spread of the gospel, the outcome of a strong experience of the power of Christ in his own heart and life. He knew a very close relationship with the Lord Jesus, and much of his teaching to us younger workers were along that line. He would say to us, "If we are to make progress in this work we must be lovers of the Lord; we must have Jesus as our portion and take time day by day to sit at his feet and hear

his Word." Notwithstanding poor health and a far from robust physical frame, his labors and self-denial were truly great and furnished an example full of inspiration to all who knew him.

4. Another secret of his influence amongst us lay in his great sympathy and thoughtful consideration for the welfare and comfort of those about him. The high standard of self-sacrifice and toil which he ever kept before himself never made him lacking in tenderness and sympathy toward those who were not able to go as far as he did in these respects. He manifested great patience and tenderness towards the failures and shortcomings of his brethren and was thus able in many cases to help them to reach a higher plane of devotion.

5. Lastly, Mr. Taylor, I observed, had a constant fear lest by degrees the Mission should lose that closeness of touch with the people which characterized its early years and which is so essential to the highest blessing on our work in a country like this. He would often warn us against the tendency to establish "a little England" of our own in the station, from which the Chinese were shut out, whilst we at the same time were losing power to understand and help them.

We all recognize that these are points that will tell in the lives of every servant of God working in China, and I trust that it may be helpful to us to be reminded of them as exemplified in the life of the founder of this Mission. Is there not a danger in the present day of laying so much emphasis on the importance of imbuing the Chinese with the Western point of view as to lose sight of the necessity of ourselves understanding theirs?

Cooperation of the China Inland Mission

It is generally known that the China Inland Mission is composed of workers drawn from different countries, denominations, and walks in life; in these particulars it is highly heterogeneous. That this tends to render cooperation between the members more difficult may be admitted. On the other hand, if such cooperation can be realized, the resultant life and action will be the component parts. Further, it is good for character to learn to adapt ourselves to the habits and thoughts of those with whom previously we have had little, if any, contact. The prejudices, often mistaken for principles, which lead people to overvalue their own ways and undervalue those of others are generally the result of restricted experience and a narrow outlook. Their removal, or at least their mitigation, is an essential part of education. Hence, what at first sight may appear to be a drawback in the personnel of the China Inland Mission proves, when taken in the right spirit, to be a means of good and of enlargement. It is obvious that at the basis of any active organization there must be a common stock of objective belief, aim, and method. In the case of missions, the ecclesiastical order and doctrinal tenets of a given denomination generally furnish the pattern. This means that, in some instances, liberty of thought and practice are restricted in respect of ecclesiastical order, considerable diversity of theological thought being permitted; in others, the reverse may be the case. Whatever abstract objections may be made to such arrangements, in practice they safeguard the convictions and provide for the religious liberty of widely varying types of workers. If, for example, a member of one denominational mission who embraced the ecclesiastical tenets of another were, in the name of religious liberty, to be allowed to modify the church order of the former, the real result would be an infringement of the religious liberty of those who started or joined the organization on the understanding that its church order was to be of a certain type. The one whose views have altered is perfectly free to join some other organization in harmony with those views, or to work independently. He cannot, in reason, expect that the convictions of those abiding by the original understandings of the mission should be sacrificed on his account. Hence the practical advantage of having a variety of organizations, each of which admittedly only covers a limited area of conviction and order. The alternative would seem to be either a fixed central authority for the whole Christian movement, under which liberty of thought and independence of action become atrophied; or virtual anarchy, breeding confusion and ending in dissolution. The blessings of cooperation are great and various. They are, however, obtained too dearly at the expense of conscientious convictions. It is true that any form of cooperation requires some sacrifice of individual thought and preference; but that is a different matter from the stifling of conscientious belief. This is not a question of charity but of keeping a good conscience. It is of little use for me to tell my friend that the matters about which we differ are really immaterial. That may be true enough as I view them; but I must, in justice, to say nothing of charity, respect his right conscientiously to view them as essential.

In the case of the China Inland Mission, the foregoing principles find their expression in a common understanding as to doctrine, which, in the light of present day thought and speculation, may be regarded as strict and conservative; whilst in respect of denominational tenets, it allows full liberty within the compass of the generally recognized churches of ecclesiastical bodies of Protestant Christendom. The Mission has not a full, comprehensive creedal statement of its own. That would hardly be consistent with its interdenominational character. It simply interprets certain great doctrines of the Christian faith, in what has been recognized by all the great denominations as the strictly conservative and evangelical sense. These doctrines are:

1. The divine inspiration and consequent authority of the whole canonical Scriptures.
2. The doctrine of the Trinity.
3. The fall of man, his consequent moral depravity and his need of regeneration.
4. The atonement through the substitutionary death of Christ.

5. The doctrine of justification by faith.
6. The resurrection of the body, both in the case of the just and the unjust.
7. The eternal life of the saved and the eternal punishment of the lost.

It may be added that, in view of present-day ambiguity of thought and language, the directors and councils of the Mission have recently thought it well to reaffirm their agreement with the strictly conservative and evangelical interpretation of the above, as stated by Mr. Hudson Taylor, with the concurrence of the councils of the Mission, at the time of his retirement from the office of general director at the end of 1902.

This feature of the Mission clearly involves a marked restriction of its membership in some directions, at the same time imparting to it a largely homogeneous character, both in respect of doctrinal belief and the type of personal piety within it.

The Mission being interdenominational, the church preferences of its members are respected, each worker being sent to a district where his views prevail. In this way, Episcopalians, Presbyterians, Baptists, Methodists, and Congregationalists are able to work within the fellowship of the Mission without compromise of conviction. Experience shows that practical unity is best secured by frankly recognizing and providing for differences of view. Attempts, however well meant, at an outwardly closer union, which either ignore or suppress sincere belief lead, later on, either to disruption or to that deterioration, intellectual and moral, due to trifling with conviction.

Most people will agree that, after all, the question of cooperation is sometimes most acute as between workers in the same station or district. It is, indeed, only in so far as the Christian spirit prevails that these relationships can be maintained as they should be. Here, as in other matters, it is the spiritual that is the truly practical. It is only by giving secret prayer and the devotional study of Holy Scripture their due time and place in the program of each day that a Christian worker can be maintained and renewed in that living fellowship with his brethren. We are so made that it takes time for us to receive the correction and the inspiration which the Spirit of God is prepared to give us. The words of our Lord to his disciples, "The kingdom of God is within you," are still true. Perhaps the most dangerous result of neglecting sedulously to cultivate the personal Christian life is that the one affected is largely insensible to the loss of tone and quality of his personality which may be painfully evident to others. It is a commonplace to say that prayer and secret devotion are important: too often, however, we virtually contradict the words by adding that it is impossible to find time for them. This simply means that, as a matter of fact, we do not regard them as of the first importance. As a rule, we allow at least an hour and a half in the day for the nourishment of our bodies. Why should we expect our Christian life to be strong and helpful to others if less time is given to secret devotion? "How shall we escape, if we neglect so great salvation?" The more we pray, the more we want to pray; the converse is also true. This often means cutting out of our schedule things which, good in their way, are taking the place of the best and highest. Fasting, the need of which was on more than one occasion emphasized by our Lord, is not necessarily to be restricted in bodily food. One of its advantages is that additional time is thus gained for waiting upon God, and we may be sure that as we thus give practical evidence of our desire to draw nigh to him, he, in his grace, will not fail to draw nigh to us.

Buy online at our website: **www.KingsleyPress.com**
Also available as an eBook for Kindle, Nook and iBooks.

Also from Kingsley Press:

AN ORDERED LIFE
AN AUTOBIOGRAPHY BY G. H. LANG

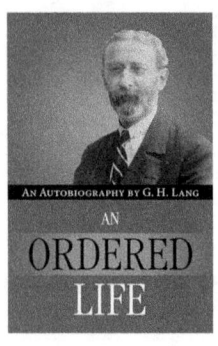

G. H. Lang was a remarkable Bible teacher, preacher and writer of a past generation who should not be forgotten by today's Christians. He inherited the spiritual "mantle" of such giants in the faith as George Müller, Anthony Norris Groves and other notable saints among the early Brethren movement. He traveled all over the world with no fixed means of support other than prayer and faith and no church or other organization to depend on. Like Mr. Müller before him, he told his needs to no one but God. Many times his faith was tried to the limit, as funds for the next part of his journey arrived only at the last minute and from unexpected sources.

This autobiography traces in precise detail the dealings of God with his soul, from the day of his conversion at the tender age of seven, through the twilight years when bodily infirmity restricted most of his former activities. You will be amazed, as you read these pages, to see how quickly and continually a soul can grow in grace and in the knowledge of spiritual things if they will wholly follow the Lord.

Horace Bushnell once wrote that every man's life is a plan of God, and that it's our duty as human beings to find and follow that plan. As Mr. Lang looks back over his long and varied life in the pages of this book, he frequently points out the many times God prepared him in the present for some future work or role. Spiritual life applications abound throughout the book, making it not just a life story but a spiritual training manual of sorts. Preachers will find sermon starters and illustrations in every chapter. Readers of all kinds will benefit from this close-up view of the dealings of God with the soul of one who made it his life's business to follow the Lamb wherever He should lead.

Buy online at our website: **www.KingsleyPress.com**
Also available as an eBook for Kindle, Nook and iBooks.

GIPSY SMITH
HIS LIFE AND WORK

This autobiography of Gipsy Smith (1860-1947) tells the fascinating story of how God's amazing grace reached down into the life of a poor, uneducated gipsy boy and sent him singing and preaching all over Britain and America until he became a household name in many parts and influenced the lives of millions for Christ. He was born and raised in a gipsy tent to parents who made a living selling baskets, tinware and clothes pegs. His father was in and out of jail for various offences, but was gloriously converted during an evangelistic meeting. His mother died when he was only five years old.

Converted at the age of sixteen, Gipsy taught himself to read and write and began to practice preaching. His beautiful singing voice earned him the nickname "the singing gipsy boy," as he sang hymns to the people he met. At age seventeen he became an evangelist with the Christian Mission (which became the Salvation Army) and began to attract large crowds. Leaving the Salvation Army in 1882, he became an itinerant evangelist working with a variety of organizations. It is said that he never had a meeting without conversions. He was a born orator. One of the Boston papers described him as "the greatest of his kind on earth, a spiritual phenomenon, an intellectual prodigy and a musical and oratorical paragon."

His autobiography is full of anedotes and stories from his preaching experiences in many different places. It's a book you won't want to put down until you're finished!

Buy online at our website: **www.KingsleyPress.com**
Also available as an eBook for Kindle, Nook and iBooks.

MEMOIRS OF DAVID STONER

Edited by
William Dawson & John Hannah

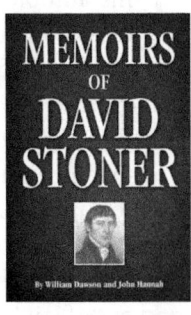

The name of David Stoner (1794-1826) deserves to be ranked alongside those of Robert Murray McCheyne, David Brainerd and Henry Martyn. Like them, he died at a relatively young age; and like them, his life was marked by a profound hunger and thirst for God and intense passion for souls. Stoner was saved at twelve years of age and from that point until his untimely death twenty years later his soul was continually on full stretch for God.

This book tells the story of his short but amazing life: his godly upgringing, his radical conversion, his call to preach, his amazing success as a Wesleyan Methodist preacher, his patience in tribulation and sickness, and his glorious departure to be with Christ forever. Many pages are devoted to extracts from his personal diary which give an amazing glimpse into the heart of one whose desires were all aflame for more of God.

Oswald J. Smith, in his soul-stirring book, *The Revival We Need*, wrote the following: "Have been reading the diary of David Stoner. How I thank God for it! He is another Brainerd. Have been much helped, but how ashamed and humble I feel as I read it! Oh, how he thirsted and searched after God! How he agonized and travailed! And he died at 32."

You, too can be much helped in your spiritual life as you study the life of this youthful saint of a past generation.

"Be instant and constant in prayer. Study, books, eloquence, fine sermons are all nothing without prayer. Prayer brings the Spirit, the life, the power." —*David Stoner*

Buy online at our website: **www.KingsleyPress.com**
Also available as an eBook for Kindle, Nook and iBooks.

ANTHONY NORRIS GROVES
SAINT AND PIONEER
by G. H. Lang

Although his name is little known in Christian circles today, Anthony Norris Groves (1795-1853) was, according to the writer of this book, one of the most influential men of the nineteenth century. He was what might be termed a spiritual pioneer, forging a path through unfamiliar territory in order that others might follow. One of those who followed him was George Müller, known to the world as one who in his lifetime cared for over ten thousand orphans without any appeal for human aid, instead trusting God alone to provide for the daily needs of this large enterprise.

In 1825 Groves wrote a booklet called *Christian Devotedness* in which he encouraged fellow believers and especially Christian workers to take literally Jesus' command not to lay up treasures on earth, but rather to give away their savings and possessions toward the spread of the gospel and to embark on a life of faith in God alone for the necessaries of life. Groves himself took this step of faith: he gave away his fortune, left his lucrative dental practice in England, and went to Baghdad to establish the first Protestant mission to Arabic-speaking Muslims. His going was not in connection with any church denomination or missionary society, as he sought to rely on God alone for needed finances. He later went to India also.

His approach to missions was to simplify the task of churches and missions by returning to the methods of Christ and His apostles, and to help indigenous converts form their own churches without dependence on foreign support. His ideas were considered radical at the time but later became widely accepted in evangelical circles.

Groves was a leading figure in the early days of what Robert Govett would later call the mightiest movement of the Spirit of God since Pentecost—a movement that became known simply as the Brethren. In this book G. H. Lang combines a study of the life and influence of Anthony Norris Groves with a survey of the original principles and practices of the Brethren movement.

The Christian Hero
A Sketch of the Life of Robert Annan

If you've never heard of Robert Annan of Dundee, otherwise known as "the Christian Hero," prepare to be astounded at the amazing grace of God in his life as you turn the pages of this incredible little biography. Its thrilling story will stir you to the depths and almost certainly drive you to your knees with an increased desire to be used for God's glory.

The record of his beginning years reads much like that of John Newton—a life of wandering far from God in the ways of sin and rebellion. At least once he miraculously escaped death through the overruling providence of God. As time passed, he became thoroughly discontented with his sinful life; but he didn't want anything to do with God or Christianity. He thought he could overcome sin and live a morally good life by his own efforts. He soon discovered, however, that he was no match for sin or Satan; and casting himself entirely on God's grace and mercy in Jesus Christ, he was gloriously saved.

From the very first day of his conversion, he became a tireless seeker of lost souls. He worked during the day time as a stone mason, but his evenings and weekends were spent preaching in the streets or in homes. Frequently he would spend whole nights in secret prayer, pleading at the throne of grace for lost sinners. As he went to his employment in the early mornings, he would often write Scripture verses on the pavement for others to read as they passed by on their way to work or school. Thus he was instant in season and out of season, using every opportunity to present to men the claims of Jesus Christ and the reality of heaven, hell, and the judgment that awaits every human soul.

Read his story and be amazed, remembering that what God did for Robert Annan he can and will do for anyone.

Buy online at our website: **www.KingsleyPress.com**
Also available as an eBook for Kindle, Nook and iBooks.

www.ingramcontent.com/pod-product-compliance
Lightning Source LLC
LaVergne TN
LVHW051048080426
835508LV00019B/1764